TORGNY SOMMELI[

THE IRON GATE
OF ILLYRIA

Translated from the Swedish by

NAOMI WALFORD

ROY PUBLISHERS, NEW YORK

LIBRARY OF CONGRESS CATALOG CARD NUMBER : 55-9148

Printed in England by
ADLARD AND SON LIMITED
London and Dorking

*This book is dedicated to some of the best people I
have ever met: my Communist friends and those who
feared, hated or were indifferent to Communism:
the Yugoslavs*

CONTENTS

I

II

III

ILLUSTRATIONS

THE IRON GATE OF ILLYRIA

PART I

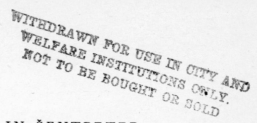
1. SNOW IN ŠENTPETER

HAVE you been to Šentpeter? Snow sweeps across the platform and the wind has prickles like a startled hedgehog. Dawn is grey. Children hop like sparrows to keep warm. Such is Šentpeter, a shrunken village in Slovenia. Here the railway from Trieste splits in two; one line leads to Zagreb, but the other runs down to Rijeka. Is there sunshine in Rijeka?

I shivered for some hours at Šentpeter while the train was battling with the snow somewhere down the line. It was a day in early January – an early hour of an early day – and when the children had stopped jumping about, they fought so as not to freeze. Snow lay like white gaiters on the line.

It was thus I met Yugoslavia: in a dirty station-restaurant, where Tito's portrait hung crooked, where the walls had deep plaster scars and the tablecloths were stained with wine and thick, loathsome sauce. The cold crept in through the door of the waiting-room, and the 10-watt bulbs in the ceiling could not pierce the gloom. I was chilled through and through – we all were – and a man from Rijeka who was reading a sporting paper shivered over the Belgrade football results. No one asked me what I wanted to eat, but a woman who had forgotten the world and whom the world had forgotten brought in a goulash that was mostly sick-coloured sauce, and a cup of tea that tasted thickly of rum. She brought in bread, tough brown bread. The man with the sporting paper looked at me and made signs to say that the summer drought had taken the harvest. We ate while snow curtained the dirty windows with white; we waited for the train from Zagreb to Rijeka that was overdue; we had goulash, brown bread and tea laced with rum.

Out on the platform the schoolchildren fought and hopped like sparrows.

I was bound for India. In Trieste, on the morning I caught the train for the frontier, it was raining; and only those who have been in Trieste when it rains know what rain is. The customs officer had no buttons on his tunic. He counted my money.

'How much? Any dollars or Swiss francs?'

'A few dollars. Some Swiss francs.'

'A few! I could live on that for a year — a lifetime.'

He clapped me on the shoulder and vanished into the corridor. The train jerked forward. As we crossed the frontier the rain came heavier and heavier, then whiter and whiter. It was snow.

At first the ground was grey, then white, and when the snow lay like a sheet over the embankment the door opened once more. The customs man had returned. He shook his head.

'It's cold — damn cold. Go to Rijeka: there are palm-trees there, and sunshine.'

And so I dumped my luggage out on to the snowy platform of Šentpeter; and if you should ever go to Šentpeter in the dawn of one of the first days of January, you will see schoolchildren sparrow-hopping in the cold, and a traveller on his way to India or somewhere sitting in a gloomy restaurant gulping sauce, and tea laced with bad rum.

An anguished whistle. A yellowish light gliding across the window-panes, and in two seconds the restaurant was empty and the children had pitched their rucksacks through the carriage-windows. The stationmaster had pulled off his wet boots and hung them up over a glowing, reeking stove, and I suppose dozed off in his chair; at any rate the train pulled away without any starting-signal. It glided down in wide sweeps through the twilight; the twilight thinned, the snow pulled up its roller-blind, below us the ground fell away and suddenly the sea was blue. The man reading the sports news laughed and pointed and let down the window. Spring was in the air.

Mostar: spring sunshine on the drain.

Bread and circuses: bread-queue in a Bosnian village, and *below*: festival in Priština.

'There's Rijeka. That's where I live!' He threw out his newspaper and it whirled away in a cascade of smoke. Then the door of the compartment slammed open and two men in blue uniforms – 'Cops', whispered the man who had thrown away his paper – and two policemen in blue uniforms, wearing big leather holsters, stood in the doorway jerking their thumbs.

There were five of us in the compartment; the others took out their grimy identity-cards and I fished up my passport. The policemen thumbed card after card. My passport they examined narrowly, first upside down and then downside up.

'You'd better come along,' they said.

Not to me, but to a woman who had been sitting hunched up in a corner. Silently she rose and stumbled out into the corridor. She never came back for her mittens. But the train stopped; we had steamed into a station where sunshine glittered on rails and platforms. The station was Rijeka.

Once outside the station I realized that I had left one world that morning, and had now arrived in another. I had left Trieste, an ant-heap full of semaphoring policemen on point-duty, cars ramming each other at street-corners, bars, and electric signs that winked green-eyed on misty nights: STOCK . . . STOCK . . . STOCK . . . But here there was not a single car — not even a taxi.

'Taxi! Taxi!'

'It's gone, but it may be back in an hour.'

'What about a tram?'

'Tram? It's a long time since any tram ran on those lines. But we have a trolley-bus that goes as far as Opatija, half-way to Abbazia. You're going to Opatija, of course.'

'Not today. Another time, perhaps.'

The street leading down to the town was broad and empty and since there were no cars to dodge we walked down the middle of it, I and my *sluznik*: a ruffian with his cap over one ear and chewing-tobacco on his moustache. He pulled my luggage along on his little handcart, muttering the whole time, 'Hotel Bonavia, Hotel Bonavia.'

'What sort of a hotel is that?'

'Very good hotel — best in Rijeka. Category B. The best anywhere. Only rich Englishmen. Rich Amerikanski too. And Party VIPs, of course. Plenty money. Plenty money.'

'How much is a room there?'

'Three hundred. Perhaps six hundred. It was worse before the New Year; tourists had to pay three times as much as we did. You're in luck, *gospodin*. They did away with that rule the day before yesterday.'

'Even so, that's too expensive for me. Is there no other?'

'No, no!' He halted and sat down on his barrow. 'Tourists must put up at the Hotel Bonavia and nowhere else.'

I eyed him. He didn't look like one of Ranković's secret police, or as if he had orders to round up all foreigners at the station and deliver them to wherever the State had set up its check-point. We had paused in front of a café, and signing to my *sluznik* to wait I slipped in and ordered a cup of coffee. They served it *à la turque*, in a little copper cup with a long stem, and with it went a glass of water. It was sweet, and the further south one went – the nearer to the once Turkish Skoplje – the sweeter it became.

I stood and drank it at the bar. The waiter was Italian and he examined my shoes first; perhaps he had been a shoe-black. Then his gaze moved upwards; when it reached my hair he wiped his thumb on a coat that once, long ago, had been white.

'You're beginning life at the wrong end, signore.' He shivered. 'What a winter! The cold! Who wants to live in cold like this, signore?'

'I'm not staying,' I said.

'Ah, you're going on to Belgrade.' And in a whisper, 'Business?'

'Much further than that — and no business.'

'Perhaps as far as Skoplje — or Greece?'

'No, to Turkey — to India.'

'Fantastic, signore! A long way ... But you must come back — you must see Opatija. Ah, Opatija in the summer! Beautiful, soft women. Dance-bands playing day and night. Flashy English sports cars with huge radiators. Although — ' and he cleared his throat, 'it's not what it was before the war.'

He looked down at the bar counter.

'But Tito's boy – you know, the one that lost his arm in Russia – he used to turn the whole place upside down. Drank like a fish and fought like a bull. You should have seen him arriving here, with all his mistresses and cars! Well, he was a general – or at least a colonel – and Tito's son, so no one could say anything. No one dared to. Those orgies! He used to throw out the waiters and smash the plates. It was a national scandal. The press kept quiet – they never print anything worth reading – but it was the kind of thing you get to hear about all the same. One day the lunatic charged the traffic head-on at a one-way bridge, in Belgrade. Full speed, mind you. The police stopped the car and out tumbles Tito's boy, roaring drunk, telling them he's commander-in-chief of the army, or something, and unless the police gave way he'd have a word with Josip himself — and then they'd be sorry. It got round to Tito, and then the balloon went up. The boy was thrown out, and he has never set foot in the White House, Tito's residence, from that day to this. But some people say that wasn't the only reason — no, nor the most important. The fact was, the youngster had been brought up in Russia, and when the question of breaking with Russia came up, in 1949, he sided with the Cominform. Tito suspected he might prove a dangerous opponent. Another coffee, signore?'

He glanced round.

'Well, that's the sort of thing we talk about among ourselves, but never aloud, remember. And don't forget what I said: come back in the summer and stay at Opatija.'

Just then a peroxide blonde walked in from the café. I took her for twenty-five, but she said she was eighteen.

'Will you stand me a coffee, too?'

When she had drunk it she said,

'Will you buy me a vermouth?'

'I can't,' I said. 'My porter's waiting outside.'

She went over to the window and looked out.

'I know him. He's asleep on your baggage; he won't wake yet awhile.'

I ordered two glasses of vermouth and we went into the café. It was a big, dark place where chairs and tables jostled one another and the walls were covered with mirrors. But the mirrors were overgrown and stuffing protruded from the chairs like entrails. I drew my finger across the tabletop; it left a broad track.

'That's where I live,' she said, pointing to the end of the mark. 'And you live right over there.' Her finger followed the line.

'Are you a Communist?' I asked, and then I saw what I hadn't noticed before: that she was pretty.

She made a startled denial:

'No, no!'

'But how do you like Tito?'

'I like all men,' she said, and was silent for a few seconds. 'I know where you can sleep for a hundred and twenty dinars.'

'Splendid,' I said. 'And are you included in the price?'

'What, as cheap as that? But you can take me to the cinema tonight.'

She held my fingers and looked at them.

We went out and woke my *sluznik*.

'To the Hotel Bonavia, Hotel Bonavia —'

But Marija slipped fifty dinars into his pocket and he turned down a side-street. We stopped at a house that seemed to be collapsing from rickets. The stairs were spiral and lopsided and the light didn't work. A sunken-cheeked woman received us and I was shown into a big room — big and cold. A double bed stood in the middle and faded family photographs hung on the walls.

'My husband was killed in the war,' said the woman. 'I have this room and a little pension to live on. We won't fill in a registration form; I'm not sure that I'm allowed to take in foreigners.'

She had four children, two born before her husband died and two afterwards; they slept in the kitchen and she in the entrance lobby. I gave the children twenty dinars each to buy sweets with, and to Marija a thousand-dinar note for the cinema tickets.

'They cost sixty dinars each. You shall have the change later.' She scampered downstairs and I was convinced that I'd lost a thousand dinars. I washed at the sink, lather frothing over potato-peelings. Through the kitchen I came out onto a terrace. On the left was the privy, a shed where four fat, wakeful hens were roosting with flash-lamps for eyes.

I went to the cinema with little hope – it was dark now, and no Stock-neons winked as in Trieste – but Marija was waiting.

'Oh good, you've come,' she said. 'I thought you'd forgotten me.'

She gave me my ticket. The seats were all sold out; it was an American Western.

'It's always full up here,' Marija told me. 'Two or three years ago they showed nothing but Russian films — the most frightful tripe. But now we get Yank pictures everybody comes.'

She put eight hundred and eighty dinars into my pocket, cautiously, without anyone seeing, and slipped a big sweet into my mouth. We shoved our way into the balcony.

'Not along the Ulica Titova,' said Marija when we came out. We crept along back alleys and when a shadow appeared before us she thrust me into a doorway.

'Look out for the police,' she whispered, 'they're everywhere.'

But the shadow passed with heavy tread.

'I'd better go,' said Marija. 'I've got to get back to the café where we met. But you mustn't come; it's no place for you.'

And Marija, the first Yugoslav I ever knew, kissed me quickly on the cheek, whispered *dovidjenja* and ran off on light, clicking soles. I stood where I was, my cheek still warm from her lips, and then went slowly down towards the town. I tried to make out her short white gaberdine coat in the darkness, but she had vanished.

21

In the solitude that was suddenly mine I first found a little restaurant in a side-street. There were fishing-nets and glass floats hanging from the roof. A fat guitar-player sat on one of the tables and sang and the customers, fishermen and seamen, all joined in the chorus. They wore caps and their hands were black with engine-oil. A huge man stood on a chair to shout down the rest; but he overbalanced and fell, and where he fell he lay.

I went out and walked down the Ulica Titova, but saw no Marija. The air was as cold as crushed ice and it bit my cheeks. The palms by the quayside shivered. Just before midnight I crossed a black canal into Sušak, the twin town. There I found a café where there was music. The violinist was playing a Paganini sonata. There were plenty of tarts there, but no Marija. And so ended my first day in Yugoslavia.

Next morning the sun was shining. It shone over the sea. Winter, but a warm, mild day in winter. The night, cold and bronchial, was forgotten. I sat on the quay surveying this curious world. A few rusty boats lay under the cranes, and a slim American six-thousand-tonner was frothing away towards the island of Krk. The sun tickled the noses of the palm-trees, but the people were grey. A few soldiers were patrolling the edge of the quay with tommy-guns slung over their shoulders, muzzle downwards. No one smiled. Queer that someone should have laughed beside me last night in the cinema.

This was like coming to a town that had a thin layer of sterile dressings over roofs and streets. People were neuters and many women wore men's trousers and jackets with broad, padded shoulders.

I thought of the Fiume that had been the Trieste of the first post-war period; the Fiume that, kindled by the torch of d'Annunzio's speeches, declared war on Italy to gain its independence. No one here mentioned d'Annunzio's heroic march on Fiume on a September day in 1919. Here was no memorial, no street bearing that visionary's name. And when, carrying a letter of introduction from the Yugoslav mission in Trieste, I asked Kazmir Sanjin to give a broadcast talk about d'Annunzio on Radio Rijeka, he began telling me how liberal an allowance of Italian-language broadcasting hours he had been given.

'Wonderful tolerance,' he said.

He said more. He told of children nailed to church walls by Italian bayonets. When I asked if that was true he said, 'If you don't believe me, go to Zagreb and find out whether I'm lying. And you'll hear more than that. You can find out all you want to know. It might be useful to you, if you're thinking of writing home to Sweden about Tito's Yugoslavia.'

In my ears was a whisper saying Dubrovnik. Dubrovnik, it said, palm-trees, eternal spring, a city that is a museum, its every stone a work of art . . . Dubrovnik was two days away by boat through the Dalmatian archipelago. But I postponed this stage of my journey to India and called on Putnik, that remarkable State tourist-bureau whose Rijeka branch was housed in the town's only skyscraper; Putnik, the traveller's constant companion whom he is compelled to trust but never can; Putnik who arranges everything and muddles most of it. Putnik means last year's time-table, dud tickets, unquoted dollar rates.

I was given a ticket to Zagreb for the through train which was said to leave in the morning.

'And while you're waiting you can visit Opatija,' said the Putnik man, giving me a sour look because I had roused him from his hibernation.

The road to Opatija runs along the coast. At first I trudged some way along the Trieste road, which was broad and smooth and very fine; I should add that it had been built by the Italians, before the war. Then the Trieste road turned off and up through Istria, while the one to Opatija continued along the coast between luxury villas with shuttered windows – memorials of capitalists shot or fled – and overgrown gardens. On walls, buildings and hoardings were red and white letters: *Živio Tito* — Long live Tito. Once there had been Long

23

Live Great Britain, USA and USSR as well, but those inscriptions were now faded and scrubbed out.

Cliffs plunged down into the water, and across the waves the tunny-fishers' ladders thrust out their springy diving-boards. But when I came to Opatija, the Istrian summer paradise of the travel-brochures – where hotels strive to outshine one another, with their swollen if empty bellies – it began to rain.

Grey rain drummed on the roofs. It pattered on terraces dreaming of last summer's dance-steps, on terraces awaiting the springy feet of the summer to come. On kisses left behind; on kisses that found no lips; on next summer's kisses. On wishes still in labour; on boats rocking in the harbour. On the tavern in the square by the harbour; on the wet place that is the square in front of the tavern by the harbour.

It was raining. Someone was weeping and the tears widened to rings on the water, then sank to the bottom. And in the tavern sat a man with a suitcase bearing hotel-labels from the four corners of the world; someone who, shadowlike, had come too early and too late to a watering-place in winter.

But next day I went on to Zagreb, and the Yugoslav adventure had begun. Rain-mist thickened to milk-mist, and out of the milk fell snowflakes, denser and denser, in millions and billions. At the station sparrows were hopping about in the snow and if one looked at them closely they resembled schoolchildren trying to keep warm. But when we had puffed up into the mountains our engine broke through the clouds and sent a flourish of smoke in joyful greeting to the blue sky. Below us lay the hills; a gnarled and twisted landscape.

2. MAN WITH THICK SPECTACLES

THE train had climbed into rarefied air that felt both light and drowsy. The rail-joints thudded, ruminant, beneath the wheels. There were four or five of us in the compartment; they snored as we clattered towards the capital of Croatia. Two big eyes surveyed me from the opposite seat, enlarged to blue globes by thick lenses. The eyes never moved, merely stared. Below them a narrow nose and below that again the lips, thin but soft. Fingers played with an overcoat-button. A leather briefcase lay on the seat; its flap fell back to reveal the whiteness of thick bundles of papers within.

'So you're going to Zagreb,' said the lips. 'I see you're a journalist.' Transparent fingers handed me a bag of round, acid sweets. It occurred to me that my typewriter lay on the baggage-rack above; it was a drawback to be thus labelled.

'Are you going to write about Yugoslavia? I'll give you an address. Look in at the Ministry of Information: they'll tell you all you want to know.'

He scrawled an address on a piece of paper and added a personal greeting.

'What do you think of our country? Peculiar, isn't it?' There was a sour note in his voice as he added, 'Very peculiar. Rather different from what you're used to.'

'Are you a Communist?' I asked.

'That's a foolish question,' said the big, blank eyes. 'But if you liked the sweets, have another.'

He held out the bag; I took one and he took one, and then he unwound the wrapping-paper. This he held up to me and I read Josip Kraš in golden letters.

'Josip Kraš,' he said. 'Do you know who that is?'

'The factory-owner,' I suggested unthinkingly. He gave a short laugh.

'The factory-owners are those who work there, the producers. But Josip Kraš was a hero of the people who died with the Partisans. Though it's true that the sweets tasted better before the war.' He put them back in his pocket. 'Neither you nor I smoke; we eat sweets instead.'

He picked up a paper and began to read, expecting no comment from me. The door of the compartment slid open for the routine inspection of papers. The rail-joints thudded. The passengers relapsed into their rhythmic snorings. I wiped the steamy window, making my hand wet, and looked out. All that flowed past was white and grey. I felt someone was watching me.

'So you're going to write about Yugoslavia! I suppose you realize you've taken on a hopeless job? What can you put down except impressions? And what are impressions but impressions?

'What do you know of us? You, coming in from outside with all your prejudices — how can you understand what's going on here? *Why* it's going on? Why it must? Do you really imagine you can form an objective opinion?

'I suppose you do. You're all the same, you journalists. We know you. You come here with your typewriters, and dash about the country in boats and trains and planes and cars — and after a fortnight of that you go home and write a book called "The Truth about Yugoslavia."

'The truth about Yugoslavia can't be caught like that. Everything's more complicated and mixed up here than it is anywhere else. What do you know, for instance, of the language problem: our three main languages, the minority languages and all the dialects? And that's only one thing.

'What do you know of our history, our six states and peoples — of the Macedonians and Montenegrins, of the antagonism between Serbs and Croats? You must give yourself time — and at the end of that time you'll only understand that you don't understand. Why? Because you haven't our blood in your veins.'

I made no protest.

'I shall only jot down a few quick impressions of my journey,' I said. 'And then I'm going on to India. Impressions are all I want. The camera can't lie, and I'm not colour-blind. And I've got a new ribbon in my typewriter.'

'That's lucky,' said the man with the blue balls for eyes. 'Our ribbons are beneath contempt. They fray and catch in the type.'

Zagreb met me with twilight. The irony of fate thrust me into a hotel called the Hotel Dubrovnik: a quasi-functional building of the thirties with a vast restaurant two floors high; on a shelf between the floors an orchestra scraped away at Viennese waltzes and the Harry Lime theme. Through the big windows I looked out over the Trg Republike — which means the Square of the Republic. At night this was a dead place where the rattle of trams was tossed between the façades of the houses. Those who visited Zagreb before the war will miss something here: an equestrian statue of the Croat governor Ban Jelačić. In the last century he helped Austria put down a nationalist revolt. As a reward he was allowed to bestride a bronze horse in the middle of the square, and the square itself was named after him.

But often during my journey through Yugoslavia I was to meditate upon the ephemeral nature of glory. What was then accounted to Governor Jelačić for merit was later to condemn him. Trg Bana Jelačića became Trg Republike, and the bronze Ban himself was hustled away into a shed. And there he remains, hoping that time will complete a half-turn of Hegel's spiral.

Early in the morning I went to the foreign department of the Ministry of Information, in Marulićev Trg. Branko Raić, the head of the department, opened his glass-fronted bookcase.

'What would you like? *Questions de Socialisme*, in twenty booklets? Tito's speech to the sixth Communist Party Congress? Youth of

Yugoslavia? *Instruction Publique en Yougoslavie*, in quarto, genuine cloth binding?'

I left Raić with a whole library under my arms.

The first days in Zagreb were dead days, stagnant days. I felt in a deep-freeze among the colourless clothes, the red star in the soldiers' caps and their panzer-grey Russian uniforms. But the stagnation was only apparent. While I was going up in the funicular to the Radićev Trg and the Old Town, watching the smoke rise over the frost-patinated roofs of Zagreb, people were playing hide-and-seek with me. Often when I returned to the hotel I found a note hanging from my room-key: 'Come to the Authors' Club at 2 p.m.' Or: 'Call on such and such an editor at four o'clock.' The vortex was drawing nearer, and I was sucked into it. Within a week I had been introduced to the cultural élite, which was not merely the intellectual group but also, and indeed chiefly, the group where opinion was formed. I was introduced to Frane Barbieri, editor-in-chief of *Vjesnik*, the biggest paper in Zagreb; to the kindly director of the Croatian National Theatre, Marijan Matković, and to leading poets such as Cecarić, Krklec, Tadijanović . . .

Then the discussions started.

We discussed Communism. Marx, as misinterpreted in the Soviet Union and realized in Yugoslavia; Stalin, the betrayer of his people, and Tito the people's friend. We discussed the Soviet leaders; and at that point someone burst out savagely,

'The criminals! It was they who betrayed socialism!'

But another said to me quietly and casually,

'There speaks one who before 1948 was the biggest Soviet boot-licker of them all."

We discussed the Five Year Plan and collective farming.

We discussed the Vatican crisis, and Orthodoxy versus Catholicism.

We discussed freedom of thought; also freedom of the Press.

We discussed and discussed. And when we had discussed we discussed all over again.

We always arrived at the same point. We talked in circles. Our starting-point was our goal, so that at last our argument became a wearisome perpetuum mobile: analytics of the closed circle, a dialectic mystique. Every question had its appointed answer. It was like a game: once one had found the key-word, no riddles remained. But the non-player stood outside and said 'Make-believe.'

'Surely you can't deny that the Yugoslav worker is the worst-paid of any in Europe?' I said.

'Ah, but wait five years, or ten. . . . Then you'll see! Only give us time. We believe in a golden future.'

This circling was like the rotation of the earth: unnoticed until the sun begins to set and night rises. Time appears to stand still, but the sudden discovery of motion makes change the more evident. In Yugoslavia, *panta rhei:* what was law one day might not be so the next. Something always happened to knock the bottom out of former truths. Yesterday the East, today the West; yesterday centralization, today decentralization. Yesterday Ivo Marković was head of the factory, today Marko Ivanović. Who will be head tomorrow? Tomorrow whose statue will be thrown down? Will Ban Jelačić be dusted off and allowed to ride out of his shed?

'I believe — we believe in a golden future,' said Zeljko Brihta, a rabid political writer on the staff of the newspaper *Vjesnik*.

I was always drawn into the circle, and from that circle there was no escape. I was swept into certain channels; there were no more than five or six, or perhaps seven of them. At any rate very few. They ran their predetermined course and there was no way out. I named these channels the Yugoslav myths. The person who led me into them often had thick spectacles, large though intelligent eyes, a narrow nose and thin, soft lips. This was the Official Man.

But at one place, where I least expected it – a place I cannot reveal – there appeared a man whose face I dare not describe.

'Forgive my bothering you,' he said, 'but I hear you're a journalist. Some of my colleagues have spoken of you. One of them said, "That

— that idiot!" I knew then that I could talk to you frankly. It's an honour to be called an idiot here. An idiot doesn't think like other people. Come on, let's go somewhere else.'

And we went somewhere else: to a park bench. It was cold but not snowing.

'I daren't say too much, for I know that even the air has ears. But this much I can say: as long as Tito's in power, so long will Yugoslavia be ruled by a dictator and so long will no one in my country feel free. Those who have come up in the world are tied by their fear of falling out of favour; the rest are silent or are silenced.

'I didn't come to you to give you a mass of material; I'd like you to get that for yourself. I've come to warn you. I felt it only right that I should. I've met a good many journalists; they come here for a week or two — or three. They're allowed to see factories, talk to well-paid workers who speak highly of the government, and to cheerful housewives who sing the praises of family allowances. Now that family allowances are being withdrawn you'll hear them praise Tito for doing away with them; because that means the State is interfering less and less in private affairs.

'Don't be like the other newspaper-men who have been here. They're given a menu, they read it, rush to the telephone and put through a call for home: "Yugoslavia is a free country! Yugoslavia is a progressive country! Yugoslavia is a democracy!"

'One thing I beg of you: beware the fancy wrappings. Notice how well everything is planned beforehand — the meticulous and detailed staff-work behind every chance incident or encounter. Notice too that whenever someone "holds other views" they are not other views in the ordinary sense; they're merely a deviation from the straight line. This is called "loyal opposition" and is encouraged for appearances' sake.

'There must always be people who protest, not discuss. Otherwise there can be no freedom.'

He glanced up at the sky. The sky was driving its clouds to pasture, in woolly flocks. He said with raised finger:

'This is the truth about Yugoslavia: it's heaven compared to what it was in 1948, but hell to what it was before the war.'

So began my journey through Yugoslavia. I thought a month would be enough, and found myself one morning on board a coasting-steamer that woke island after island in Adriatic light. I still had no fixed plans, beyond the idea that India was my goal; the boat chugged ahead at a few feeble knots and I was in no hurry. A month seemed an eternity and I should cross the Greek frontier all in good time. But when I saw the morning light kindling the waters of the archipelago to a green-blue, shimmering flame, a longing awoke in me for light over more than just these smooth-baked islands and a coast of pines.

And so I lit lamps in a room still dark. I did it planlessly. At one moment I would busy myself with the problems of collective farming; next day I stood in the Roman graveyard of Solin, where life had cut its inscriptions of mortality on the tombs. I tried also to push my way into Yugoslav folk-music, into the history and the traditions of the people. I wanted to meet people, to know how they lived. But *I* wanted to live, as well; to feel, to be a human being among the rest.

The lamps I lit burned feebly, and by their light one could not see the whole room.

I began at the wrong end. Instead of visiting first the centre, Belgrade, where everything – decentralization notwithstanding – had its roots; instead of engaging in Marxist discussions with some contributor to the newspaper *Borba* (for what was said in Zagreb could only be a watered-down version), I lay on a Dalmatian island, listening to the song of the first almond-tree to blossom there. For two months I stayed spellbound in Dubrovnik, and when I came away I thought I had no heart left.

Months had passed by then, and India lay further away than ever. I unpacked my typewriter in the light room with the patches of damp, at the Hotel Balkan in Belgrade, and again changed my character. The man who every evening in Dubrovnik had gone out to the jetty with the red lantern, and let moonlight allay the world with its serenity, became the man who, notebook in hand, sought to record every falsehood or truth about Yugoslavia: the number of radio-sets per head of the population, the clashes with the opponents of the régime, the output of iron ore before and after the break with the Soviet Union. . . .

There are different ways of absorbing a country. A country can be an intellectual experience, and also a purely emotional one. For me Yugoslavia was both. As I travelled, my pile of manuscript grew, but these rough drafts clashed with one another, because some concerned chiefly myself, while others related more to the material that was being experienced through me. And when in course of time, and in spite of many things, a book began to grow, nothing turned out as it should, and there was nothing I could do about it.

Least of all could I claim to have revealed 'The Truth about Yugoslavia.' Some said 'Yugoslavia has a population of seventeen million, and seventeen million of them love Tito.' Others declared that 'The most hated man in Yugoslavia is called Tito.' Which was right? I don't know. No one knows.

Those who want official figures and the official outlook may apply to the propaganda-shops, and like me they will be submerged in literature. But those who want to hear the voice of the people must stand in the Trg Republike one frosty misty morning, or walk at dusk along the Maršala Tita in Belgrade. They will see looks that are pro and looks that are con; but most looks and voices talk of quite other things: of the latest international football match against Belgium, of the neighbour's wife who has found a lover, of the price of radishes, or the holiday trip to Lake Ohrid, or to the white town on the silver-green island of Rab.

'Tell me now,' I said to a girl student in Dubrovnik, 'what do you think of Tito? Do you approve of the one-party system? Is your big army there to frighten the Russians or the Yugoslavs themselves?'

'I don't know,' she said. 'I don't think much about that sort of thing.'

Yesterday: Steps in Mostar. (*Below*) Tomorrow: Flats in Skoplje.

Market-woman of Skoplje.

'But you must,' I said. 'Can you speak up and say "I want an alternative to Communism"? Are you a free woman?'

'Perhaps not,' she answered, 'but I'm happy. I wake every morning to the smell of flowers in our garden, wafting in through the window. I throw on my clothes and hurry out, saying "Oh what a wonderful day it is and how lucky I am to be alive now, and in Dubrovnik, the most beautiful place in the world!" I wonder who I shall meet today, what will happen this evening, what flowers I shall pick. Every second is a new adventure.'

'You little egoist!' I said. 'All you bother about is yourself and your private happiness. You must work for a way out — for real freedom.'

She laughed — and she was perhaps the loveliest girl in Dubrovnik.

'I've never known of any other conditions than those we're living in. When I was little there was a war on. And now I've no time for anything but living. And I want to live. I'm happy.'

Wanting to live. To discuss not politics but football. To demand not social reforms but a bottle of wine in a tavern at Novi Bad. To allow a small clique, who have a taste that way, to handle politics. To drift through the dusk of a May evening along the Maršala Tita. To be.

The truth about Yugoslavia was not merely the question of Communism or non-Communism, but also of all the common-place alternatives of life: bananas or pastries for dessert. It was not only the *Skrupština*, the parliament in Belgrade, but also the minarets of Bosnia, and the two fishermen who lit their decoy-lights between Dubrovnik and Lokrum.

The hundred thousand who cheered the military parade in Belgrade on May Day would with equal enthusiasm have torn up newspapers and strewn them in a joyous shower if a democratic president – in the Western sense – had driven along the same streets; those streets being called of course by other names than Maršala Tita and

Bulevard Revolucije. No doubt they would have cheered King Peter and perhaps even a fascist dictator, provided he had blown his propaganda-trumpet long enough.

The masses are nothing but docile cattle, herded together by curiosity, by instinct or by a whiplash on their quarters. Never mind who holds the whip; it's the whip itself that counts, and the important thing is that it should be felt often enough to engender the myth.

Only a few want to be political freaks, to sharpen their horns and break out of the herd.

Only a few wait on a balcony with a bomb when the procession moves past below. These are the ones who deflect the current, who turn the pages of history. Gavrilo Princip. Ante Pavelić. Josip Broz Tito.

All the others want to live.

In order to present the truth one must be a historian, an ethnographer, an economist, an agricultural expert, a geologist, and many other things. Also one must stay longer than six months in the country.

But there are other places to be visited.

To present the truth one must look into the future, since conclusive truth lies unspoken in the mouth of the future.

I did not want to wait so long; for first must come the time of reassessment, and then that of probability.

Living is more important.

3. ABOUT SOMETHING ELSE

TO live. For some, to live is to travel. And as life itself is a journey, where every arrival is the starting-point for some new expedition, then to travel is to live doubly, to multiply one's starting-points, one's wayside halts and one's final destinations — which are never final.

There are two kinds of dreams about places: the dreams of places one never reached and those of places to which one never returned. With the dream begins a journey, and journeying is necessary. Some are condemned to it; for them there can be no rest. For them the strokes of the clock must always herald the next departure.

The dream of Samarkand is apprehensible and devoid of imagery: a city without houses, a desert without sand or oasis, shadows without people, people without shadows; a horizon that ever recedes. Some are sentenced to a life of hard labour, others to the electric chair. But those who are sentenced to Samarkand are condemned to seek something that is not there, and so to cross the frontier into annihilation of another kind.

One discovers too late that Samarkand never exists and exists everywhere. Too late one finds that what one has left behind is what one was looking for.

We always seek an excuse for our journey, just as we seek one for living: a tobacconists' shop, a doctor's thesis on the back legs of ants, a home with dotted curtains.

There are travellers in geology; they record in their red note-books every kind of rock that slides past the carriage window.

There are travellers in antiques; in every town they hurry to the antique-shops and fill their trunks with Moroccan brass trays and machine-turned Indian ivory elephants. . . .

There are those who travel to look at churches, whether Byzantine, Romanesque or Gothic; and those who travel to watch football matches.

That is what culture has brought us to: pretexts.

One day perhaps there will be a new journey, a journey on a simpler pretext. A day when we shall travel for the sake of travelling; and live, perhaps, for the sake of living.

He lives closest to life and death who is poised between consciousness and unconsciousness. His journey alone is hallowed who understands its importance and its unimportance; and that its unimportance is what is important. Frontier-people come nearest to the truth: those who live on the shores of great seas, those who kindle fires on peaks beneath the stars.

I have washed my feet in the blue foam of the Adriatic and seen the prints of naked feet in the eternal spring of the Atlas Mountains.

Let us despise those who cannot travel simply for the sake of moving from one place to another. The souvenir-hunters, for instance, and the specialists in church-architecture. Above all, those who try to convert sublime experience into something of inferior quality: words. Worse still, those who try to coin words into silver.

But he who travels to write will one day come to a city and find he can no longer coax secrets from its houses, nor hidden words from gardens. He will walk mute streets and the gable-ends of houses will lack faces. He will discover that today all is as it was yesterday, as it has always been: the shop-windows, the people he jostles, the trams, churches or mosques.

He will come to a city and see nothing but what he has long known: the certainty that every fly-speck of the world is the identical mirror of its core. Kisses are always the same, whether in Bulgaria or – let's jab at the map with a blind forefinger – in Perugia.

Yet writing is necessary, for those to whom writing is sailing.

There are two purposes in sailing: to sail away or to sail home.

What do Sarajevo, San Fernandino or Las Carolinas matter? It is the flight into one's own landscape that is important. Not by images of cities and seas but by viewing ourselves shall we be able to sum up our journey: we found what we were looking for, our voyage was a chain of marvellous discoveries, expected and unexpected. Or mockingly: we found everything was different, more bitter, more full of despair; or – deeper despair – we found nothing at all.

Yes, there are two aims in travel: to go away or to come home. Just as flight is a flight from or a flight to.

When will our outward landscape become our inner one — our flight from become a flight to? I went to Yugoslavia in years of transition, when all was contradiction and nothing could be clearly deciphered. Someone who had just left Dubrovnik wrote to me from Belgrade:

'Serbia, you'll find, is something quite different. All my ideas have been turned upside down and I leave this country more bewildered than ever.'

Anyone who listens one evening in Skoplje to a Macedonian folk-song will feel the pulse of Yugoslavia: a song sung in a forced voice to an accompaniment of smoothly gliding fiddle-bows, a song of uneven rhythms, an ocean where the wind blows counter to the tide and waves break their necks.

For the truth is that whatever is immature – whatever is flower but not yet fruit – will be irrational, equivocal and mysterious; like dawn over Kossovopolje and twilight over the heights of Montenegro. Like a young woman. Here is a country that has yet to find a way out of its conflicts: Yugoslavia, the land of opposites.

How could *I* grasp the truth about Yugoslavia, or present anything beyond an impressionist sketch of what I saw, learned and felt? Not even stones, houses, hills or trees reveal themselves plainly. Then one day when I was in Belgrade I had a letter from someone who had just arrived in Dubrovnik.

'I live outside the town, in Gruž. . . . Dubrovnik is so completely of stone that it hurts. I'm being ground to flour between great mill-stones.'

And I! I who had been woken every day by the market-folk beneath my window and by the morning chimes from the cathedral, to a city that was a garden, where every house was a flower, and the Placa – the place for strolling – a river of limpid water. Yet it was true that only in the gardens of the Franciscan and Dominican monasteries were there plants and trees, and that except for the orange-trees in their tubs by the Ploče gate, everything within the encircling walls was of dead white blocks of stone.

The traveller is a piece of litmus-paper. In Rome he becomes an amateur archaeologist; in Spain, sun, blood and sand. In Vienna he sits in cafés. He is incapable of breaking this chain of transformations, and if he is the aimless kind of traveller it was for these very changes that he set out. For this is the whole point of travelling: not to know what is going to happen; not to know in what way events outside the windows of the senses will be experienced within them.

Aimless people are like white blotting-paper; they must soak up what is already written, and perhaps – like blotting paper – reproduce it back to front. Such is the true traveller. Ignorant as Heidenstam but open to a spate of impressions which he canalizes through head, heart and reins.

Yugoslavia is said to have two sides: a fair Potemkin façade of Adriatic coast, where foreigners gain a one-sided impression of a land of smiles and song on moonlit quays; and an inner side of poverty and socialist experiment — the seething, eternally Balkan side. In one the individual is forced to be an animal, to live, feel and merge with marble and palms; on the other he is compelled to be abstract, to analyse and be merged in ideas — or break with them. Who in Dalmatia, so far from Belgrade, bound by the invisible chains of beauty, can see the serious side of things except through the wrong end of a telescope? Who discusses Communism on Opatija's blasphemous shores? But who, standing in the Trg Republike before a gigantic portrait of Tito, can help forgetting the murmur of palm-trees?

In Belgrade ideas lie in wait for you like troops before the assault —

but beware! Ideas are never life; they merely sway the self in one direction or another. Who can remember the day he learned the transcendental logic of Kant — still less the moment when he understood it? But the dawn of that morning when the white coasting-steamer left Rijeka — that he will remember, for it belongs to the seconds that are crystallized. Life is an instant of memory; the self is existence, certainly, but an existence outside time and space.

For those who love life, who love those instants of suspense that harden to eternal stalactite; for those who love Dubrovnik, that's to say, more than Belgrade, the Placa more than the Trg Republike, it may be painful to go forth into that Trg Republike and knock at doors, one after the other, begging to be let in; the doors of the Co-operative Association, the Trades Unions, the Ethnographical Museum, the head office of the Information Bureau, and all the other official buildings. But when I stood in the Trg Republike I certainly was not doing it because I liked it. It was as if I had been dragged there by a ring through my nose.

Perhaps a book about Yugoslavia would be saltier and more colourful if it were one-sided: if it described the journey as simply an excursion into the perils of the primitive world. But I had no choice. I had crossed the frontier aimlessly, and on a pretext: that of going to India. I was therefore as blank as new blotting-paper, and when I had left the Placa and stepped out into the Trg Republike, words were written in me backwards. I had to stay to analyse, to find a probable interpretation. And so goaded, I had to let myself be poisoned by the arsenic of statistics and political propaganda.

My way of looking at Yugoslavia was partly the result of regrettable circumstance. I travelled in the dullest and most prosaic way: by train, bus and steamer. Once I went in a taxi from the capital of Montenegro, Cetinje, to the coast town of Budva; that was a terrifying trip on wobbly wheels past dizzy, unguarded precipices. Another time I drove in a horse-drawn cab from the station at Priština, the capital of Kosmet, to the Hotel Nova Jugoslavija. Those, with a voyage down the Danube along the Iron Curtain, were the only unconventional trips I made; yet even those few whiffs of adventure, horse-dung and scorched brake-linings loaded me with material for poetic and dramatic description. What a book it might have been if I had cruised southwards in a small sailing-craft through the Adriatic archipelago, or plodded on donkey-back through villages and towns!

I should have been where the sun sets, in the mountains or among the outermost islands. I should have slept among Albanian peasants in Rugovo, eating brown bread and raw eggs bought at farms on my way. But I should never have arrived in the Trg Republike. No one can sail across the Trg Republike, and no donkey-trails lead that way.

I did not even set out with a rucksack, in the hope of thumbing a lift on a lorry for a few miles. I had crossed Norway and Sweden like that, and wandered through France, Spain and Morocco. I had slept among shielings to the music of goat-bells, in Spanish fields while donkeys brayed raucously at their watering-places, beside Moroccan roads with a dagger in my hand and above me Antares in the sign of the Scorpion. In Yugoslavia I stayed mostly at first-class hotels – since they were cheap – and complained whenever I was slightly bitten by bugs or fleas.

I always had a thousand-dinar note or so on me, and never had to repeat the experience I had in 1949, when I woke one day to find myself left behind in a village in the Atlas Mountains with eight hundred Moroccan francs in my wallet.

If at that time, in 1949, I could have seen the figure now steaming about – sometimes second class! – in trains and boats through Yugoslavia, I should never have believed it could be myself. Not only because my spectacles had been stolen in Tangier, but because I should have refused to admit the possibility of such moral decay.

If I had been compelled to recognize myself I should first have spat upon me and then said,

'*Quo vadis*, Torgny Sommelius?'

So rapidly can a man sink to philistinism.

No wonder I landed in the Trg Republike.

Only by dragging myself out by the hair could I get away from it. How many souls have been destroyed through being unable to find a way out of the market-place of politics!

I never reached India.

I never reached even the Greek frontier.

4. A CHAPTER ON FEAR

IN a small town in Bosnia, Serbia or somewhere else I met a young man, a student. It was chance that brought us together; I asked him the way, and he — he stammered. He was delighted to meet a foreigner.

To meet a foreigner, he said, was for him to meet a human being.

'I live here as if I were on an island,' he told me. 'Come along and we'll go to the tavern.' Taking me by the arm he shoved me with gentle force into a cellar and ordered two brandies. And when we'd drunk two more and yet another two, we came out into air that had suddenly turned cool.

'I live in constant dread,' said the Yugoslav. 'Before the war my father was one of the leading men of the commune. I had two sisters and a brother. My brother and one sister lived in Zagreb. They were murdered after the war by the Partisans. Don't ask me why. There was no reason for it except that someone had to die. Someone had to die for the revolution.'

He clenched his fists.

'I shall never forget it. I shall never forget it. . . .'

We met again next day, and that was the last time I saw him. He was close-lipped now, and pale. His hands shook. We sat at an outdoor café in a park. I wanted more information.

'Come, let's go,' he said.

We walked a few yards, then he turned, went back to our table and pocketed an empty film-carton I had left on it. But I wanted more information.

' — the kind of thing you told me yesterday.'

He was agitated.

'I would like to tell you everything – everything I know – but I

can't. . . . If you knew what I went through last night! I kept thinking:
it's my duty to tell it; everybody ought to know the things I've seen.
And then suddenly fear came over me and I saw the security-police
knocking at my door and ordering me to go with them. I must have
fallen asleep. I must have screamed in my sleep.'

He turned and pointed to the café. Green light flowed over the
heads of the customers. Bearded men emptied their wine-glasses, a
woman rocked a bundled-up baby in her arms and a dance-tune
from Vojvodina splashed down from loud-speakers hung in the trees.

'Some of those people have seen me with you. Among them there'll
be an informer. I can't trust anyone. Do you realize what it means to
be seen with a foreigner? That alone makes me suspect. To tell one's
story is to leave one's card.'

He held up the film-carton.

'I have to consider every action, yours and mine. You left this
behind. I had to pick it up. One day I might find myself standing in
front of a desk; behind the desk the chief interrogator; on the desk the
carton. "Do you know what this is?" he'll ask me. "No." "Then we'll
tell you. On the seventeenth of March 1953 you were with a man you
had met the day before. You went to a café where he left this carton
behind. Did you know that man was working against us, to harm us
— did you know that when you gave him information?" "I gave him
no information," I'll say. "We'll see," says the man — and then the
torture begins.'

'That was before 1948,' I objected. 'That sort of thing doesn't
happen any more.'

He smiled.

'It was worse then. That doesn't mean it's all right now.'

A path had brought us to a pool. He picked up a pebble, pushed it
into the carton and threw it in the water. When the box had sunk,
rings widened on the surface.

'I didn't sleep last night,' he said. 'At first I thought: it's my duty
to say everything – I owe it to truth – I owe it to my brother's futile
death, and my sister's. I mustn't consider my own safety — I must

speak and be prepared to suffer. At that point I felt at peace. Then the image of my parents came before me. "We have lost Marija," said father. "We have lost Petar," said mother. And mother cried and said, "We have only you left. What will become of us now?" And then I shivered. I was their only son — the prop of their old age. How could they endure it if I were put in gaol? All night I weighed my duty to avenge my brother and sister against my duty to my father and mother — and I found no answer. But today as I watched mother making the coffee for breakfast and saw father open the window, saying, "It looks like being a real spring day" – as they stood before me, real, flesh and blood – I knew I couldn't meet you again. I am sorry, because I live on an island, but I see the necessity of it. I won't take risks and bring greater sorrow on my parents. Therefore I beg of you, let someone else be the scapegoat for anything you write, but let me go free.'

He looked across the pool. Among the leaves on the far side a bird uttered a shrill cry. I asked,

'Are you afraid?'

He replied,

'Yes, I'm afraid.'

Our hands met. His was shaking. He returned along the same path; I waited for a few minutes and then found another way back to the town. But the last thing I heard was the bird's cry.

But now I shall tell another story. I shall tell the story of the shoemaker whom I met in a train or on the staircase of a hotel or somewhere else.

The shoemaker Marko Danović was a simple and rather stupid man, or so they said in his village. But he was strong and he sang as he hammered at his shoes; and so he was called the singing shoemaker. One day the war came and Marko Danović did as all the other men in his village did: he picked up a hay-fork, stabbed a German soldier to death from behind, stole his rifle and went into the woods to join the Partisans. He believed in Tito and his Partisans, but not in

Mihailović and the Chetniks. ('I saw them drinking toasts of brother-
hood with the Germans in the village inn'.) Nor in King Peter, who
had flown to London with all his ministers instead of staying at home
and fighting in the mountains.

'If anyone can sweep out these German lice, it's Tito,' said Marko.

And Tito did as Marko expected of him. Peace came, but there
was famine in the country and the American UNRRA-rations didn't
go far. Marko returned to his village, sat down on his stool and sang
songs about Tito on an empty belly: 'Why are you so pale, Comrade
Tito?'

'Wait!' said Marko. 'Tito whacked the Germans; now he'll give
us bread.' So he joined the Communist Party. For think what the
war had meant to him! Only now did he realize the injustices there
had been, and how at last they would be banished by Communism.

'Now we're all as grand as each other,' said Marko, when he gave
his customers back their shoes. 'No more upper class and lower class.
You and I are equal, comrade,' said Marko.

But years passed, bread grew dearer and the 'best comrades' in the
Party swished by in new American cars. 'Queer that they can afford
it,' thought Marko, 'when I can't even buy enough bread for my
children.'

The day came when he no longer sang, and at last he had had
enough. He threw his shoes at the wall, went to the inn and got
drunk. Afterwards he had a dim recollection of having been carried
home.

Next day he was ordered to report to the UDBA, the security
police.

'You've done yourself a bad turn, Marko Danović,' said the village
UDBA agent. 'You have accused the Party of treachery to their
ideals and to the people, you have spoken disparagingly of socialism
and you called Tito a blackguard. You are working for the enemies
of the people, Marko Danović.'

Marko wept:

'I never said anything like that. I was drunk yesterday, and — '

45

'We don't give a damn whether you were drunk or sober. Are you working for the enemies of the people? Answer yes or no.'

'No,' stammered Marko.

He was thrown into gaol. For a whole week he was given no food. But confess he would not. Then he was locked into a cupboard so narrow that he had to stand upright, and here he had to stay for another week. From time to time the door was opened and a bucket of cold water was flung over him.

'That'll help you not to fall asleep,' grinned the guard. 'For if you sleep, comrade, you'll only have bad dreams.'

Marko Danović never gave in. After six months' arrest he was released for lack of evidence.

That is the story of the shoemaker who stopped singing. Stopped singing one day in the drought-year of 1950.

'What I should like to do,' said the shoemaker, 'is this — ' His hand shot forward with a quick, sinuous movement. 'But I can't do as others do; I've got a wife and children at home. What would happen to them? So I must stay and keep my mouth shut.'

That rapid gesture was not his own. Like speech, sign-language is born of convention and elementary needs. To describe Yugoslavia without interpreting the language of the hands – in other words, to confine oneself to listening, to talking to people in ill-lit bars and on nocturnal walks along a shore-road – would be to reject an essential clue.

Every people has its language, every country its signs. Macedonian children who want to be photographed make the camera-sign, with their fingers before their eyes in a figure-8. Other signals have graver significance.

When the hands are held out from the body with the wrists crossed, only handcuffs are lacking. 'But they're not far off,' says the gesture. 'Sh — sh! There's an UDBA agent about!' Or: 'We must talk of something else.' Or: 'I was in prison.' Or: 'He's in prison.' No doubt the Romans used some galley-slave symbol.

But Marko Danović the shoemaker was evoking a snake slithering over the ground, a man slithering through barbed wire or another man flying across the sea to Italy. Or the one who fled; the one who, without a passport (passports were only for the 'reliable') found, one moonless night, a chink into the West.

Signs arise to simplify, to convey complicated events by easy symbols, or give expression to thoughts when the tongue must be still. The prison sign was necessary so long as the gates of the gaol hung open like the jaws of a ravening bloodhound. Flight would never have been symbolized by a sinuously-moving hand if only a single selfish fugitive had organized his private escape in a rowing-boat. Prison was always a terrifying reality; flight the only certain method of avoiding it.

We had made a tacit agreement, I and my good friend with whom I dined every day at the fish-restaurant in a side-street off the Placa in Dubrovnik; an agreement never to talk politics. We talked of everything else: of postage-stamps, of wind and weather, of the latest scandals, of the grimy collector of icons who went every Saturday to visit his mistress in Cavtat. One day I happened to get on to the subject of the Yugoslav press.

'These rags of newspapers you have here — are you really satisfied with them?'

He went white at my all too loud remarks and seized me by the arm, by which I knew that I had said the wrong thing. Out in the street he gasped,

'Can't you understand that I don't want to listen to that sort of talk? I haven't been interested in politics since 1940.'

Many of the foreign journalists I met avoided making friends or getting in any way involved. What contacts they may have had with the Yugoslavs had to be made surreptitiously. Thus they were free to write what they liked without risk of corrupting or compromising their acquaintance unawares. But I made many friends in the course of my six Yugoslav months. Some were enemies of the régime, some not. Some received me openly, others let me come and go by a back way through the garden. At least the time was past when every

47

Communist was a spy and informer, and people vanished without trace. The Soviet system was weakening day by day and the individual had less and less to fear. The fear I did meet with was in many cases a left-over from the age of terror when Tito held his people in a harder, more implacable grip than any other dictator behind the Iron Curtain.

Was that separation by the pool on March seventeenth unnecessary?

'Yes,' my Communist friends would have answered. 'Look at us; we're not afraid to go about with you. We show ourselves with you openly.'

'Yes, but you're Communists. They know where they are with you. What about the others who are afraid?'

'Afraid?'

'Yes, afraid. Has there never been a time of terror in Yugoslavia?'

'Never.'

'And no security-police?'

'Oh, of course — but you must understand our position. Every revolution has its enemies. A revolution that liberates the people is bound to have enemies who try to enslave them again, and introduce a fascist, capitalist dictatorship. Everyone who works against the present régime – everyone who accepts reactionary ideas, whether from East or West – is an enemy of the Yugoslav people. While a revolution is in progress, and immediately after it, it must be protected by security-police. But when it's an accomplished fact and the community has begun to progress peacefully, without disturbance — then the régime can relax its pressure. In 1945 we had to have spies, to combat capitalist conspirators. In 1948 we had to have them because Soviet Russia was doing all it could to bring the Stalin system into the country by infiltration. But in 1953 and 1954 espionage and informer methods are unnecessary.'

I met many good Communists. I also met many corrupt ones.

I met many corrupt opponents of the régime, too.

The Prisoner of Krasic: Cardinal Archbishop Alojzije Stepinac

Peace on the waters of Tragir. (*Below*) The Six Pillars of Diocletian.

I met good people and bad in Yugoslavia, as in every other country. Slothful or fanatical, or something between the two.

I met many Communists who seriously and selflessly worked for the 'golden future' they believed in.

I also met people who snoozed in their offices.

I met anti-Communists who snoozed side by side with Communists.

I met those who worshipped Tito and those who detested him.

I met those who passively resisted by not lifting a finger for the 'new socialist Yugoslavia' — but I never saw any open opposition.

I never came in contact with any underground movement.

Who could have organized it? The enemies of socialist Yugoslavia were either in concentration camps or in exile. In London, Washington, Paris or South Africa.

It was natural for Yugoslavs to bow beneath the yoke of a dictator. They had never been free; they had always been ridden on a short rein, under the knout. Does a man beg for freedom who has never known what freedom is? Are the Yugoslavs ripe for what we call freedom? They have always hated and loved their leaders, and yielded to them because they were the stronger. Many said, 'There's no alternative. First Tito beat the Germans, then the royalists and then the Stalinists. Who can beat Tito? We must accept him because he is the toughest and the most powerful. And then there's his breach with USSR. We mistrusted him until then. But now —'

The régime made mistakes, but it learned from them and acknowledged them, in accordance with good Marxian and Christian practice!

But there were also those who said, 'What can we do? There are more soldiers here than anywhere else in the world. What can one man do against ten soldiers?'

And so when I think of Yugoslavia I shall certainly remember the grey-white mountains, a frozen moonscape to which not even a shepherd can entice his flock. I shall remember the white cliffs of Dalmatia, the tall masts of the date-palms, the orange-groves, the thorny agaves, and water so glitteringly clear and still that even the bottom was transparent. I shall remember the endless plains of Serbia and the chess-playing peasants on a collective farm near Belgrade.

I shall remember that no one prevented me from seeing all this. The roads were almost unbarred, events almost unconcealed, the few attempts to pull the wool over my eyes so ill-managed and the Potemkin-décor so badly-painted that they argued against rather than for the régime. I saw all the sores and boils and all the good will. From these must arise fresh sores, or the art of healing.

I shall remember stones and flowers, deep water and the high white snow of the hills.

But I shall also remember people who lived in dread, a land of grey convicts swinging their picks on roads and railways, grey soldiers wriggling over spring meadows or beating drums and singing battle-songs through the streets of Sarajevo.

I shall remember eyes as frightened as those of deer.

5. THE CARDINAL WILL DIE IN KRASIĆ

I BELIEVE cars, like ships, are feminine; certainly this one was as capricious as any woman. Outwardly she looked like a '39 Ford, but the driver thrust his fingers under the sweat-band of his cap, scratched his head and told me that things weren't what they seemed, and that the clattering engine was in fact made up of bits from at least twenty other cars. He had put her together himself in 1945 and knew every little nut and bolt as well as he knew the letters of his name. This bundle of junk, which threatened to fall apart at any moment, laboured along the concrete road southward from Zagreb, hooting irascibly at cows, peasants and two cyclists. Zeljko Brihta, the thin boy beside me, was putting together a jigsaw puzzle in words, from which I made out the following: Dr Alojzije Stepinac, former Archbishop of Yugoslavia, Cardinal since November 29th 1952, prisoner in Krasić, the village of his birth. It was to Krasić, twenty-five miles from Zagreb, that the driver was taking us.

'Why are all foreigners so much interested in the Stepinac business?' asked Zeljko Brihta. 'Have you nothing else to worry about?'

Zeljko Brihta, political contributor to the newspaper *Vjesnik*, was a frail-looking boy with prominent ears. He was the product of a thorough-going socialist education. 'Stepinac! A traitor and fascist collaborator!' And the car that was not a Ford snorted across the plain. The plain was under water. Willows thrust clenched fists out of the lakes and the white mountain ranges on the horizon danced menacingly.

'Stepinac's a cunning devil — he knows what he's doing. And he must take the consequences.'

51

Thus spake Zeljko Brihta. One day he will sit in the Belgrade Parliament.

As we approached Krasić, Brihta told me a story, now in long sentences from an invisible book, now in short, impassioned trumpet-blasts. And this was Zeljko Brihta's story about Stepinac, the Vatican, the Fascist Party Ustaša, and Ante Pavelić.

'There's no one like Tito,' he said. 'He was the man who succeeded in reconciling Serbs and Croats. You know what it was like under the monarchy — how reactionary elements, both Serbian and Croatian, worked to bring about a split in the country. One of the criminals attacking Yugoslav unity was the fascist Ante Pavelić, who was in exile in Italy. It was Pavelić who was behind the murder of Alexander I in Marseilles in the early thirties. He boasted of it himself. The patient died, but the operation was unsuccessful. Pavelić bided his time, and in 1941 his chance came. With the Pope's blessing he arrived in Zagreb under cover of German bayonets, to found the kingdom of Croatia. Archbishop Stepinac was one of the first to shake him by the hand.

'It wasn't long before Pavelić had the Pope behind him. The papal legate Marcone arrived from Rome and accredited himself with Pavelić. Two beautiful souls found one another, just as Franco and Pius had found one another. Common interests stimulated co-operation between Stepinac and the Vatican on the one hand, and Pavelić and the Ustaša on the other. The Ustaša's aim was the foundation of an Aryan-Croatian state; that of the Vatican the conversion of Greek-Orthodox Serbs. So the campaigns were started, the Ustaša's against the Serbs, the Pope's against heresy; the first by means of the gallows and instruments of torture, the second by means of baptism. Cross and gallows on the same hill. Mass-murders were instituted in the name of Church and State. Hundreds of peasants were forcibly baptised before the altars of Glina and Bosanka-Dubica, then butchered and left to perish in the blazing churches. Only one woman escaped; she shammed dead under the heaps of bodies.'

(On my very first day in Yugoslavia the deputy-head of Radio Rijeka, Kazmir Sanjin, pointed at his head and cried, 'With my own eyes I've seen children pinned to a church wall with bayonets. I *know* that priests and Ustaša-men drank the blood of the dying Serbs, with invocations — like a religious rite. Such scenes are never forgotten; they're nailed into one's brain.')

'Now don't say this is all propaganda,' begged Zeljko Brihta. 'We have proof that it's not. Photographs that the Fascists themselves took. And remember, everything that happened was countenanced by Stepinac — I might almost say blessed by him. When the Ustaša troops marched away to murder the Partisans – their comrades, their own flesh and blood – he bade them God speed.

'But Stepinac compromised himself in other ways. If you don't believe me I'll tell you about Lisac, the Chief of Police — the Himmler of Croatia. Indeed, Himmler was a child to him. When the Partisans liberated Zagreb he fled to Austria and there continued his activities. An illegal Ustaša transmitter had been installed in Zagreb, and information was sent by it to the Ustaša group which had fled abroad. But both transmitter and code fell into Communist hands.

'The Communists used these to keep in touch with the traitors. Messages like "Things quieter now. Come back" went out, and one after the other the war-criminals were decoyed home. The police simply sat and counted all the fish as they swam into the net.

'It was in this way that Lisac was brought back. They found him hiding in the Archbishop's palace. And in the Archbishop's cellar they found a whole boxful of gold fillings taken from the teeth of murdered Serbs.

'Lisac was brought to the gallows. But Pavelić, the biggest gangster of them all, fled disguised as a monk and under a false name via the Vatican and Spain to the Argentine, where Peron gave him asylum.'

(When I returned to Zagreb I received permission from the information department to go through the so-called Ustaša file, which the Communists came upon soon after the revolution. 'You can go through it if your stomach will stand it,' said Comrade Raić. The dossier consisted of some thousands of photographs taken either by Germans or by members of the Ustaša. There were pictures of massacred women, ripped open with their entrails bursting out, and in the background a brave soldier in straddling jackboots smoking a pipe; of headless children's bodies in a ditch; of the dedication of a children's home, with Catholic priests raising their hands in the Heil-sign; of hundreds of dismembered corpses heaped on the river-bank; of heads with bloody lumps instead of eyes; of Stepinac in humble audience with Pavelić; of Serbs mustered in a church, their bundles at their feet, having been captured on the way to work, awaiting baptism and unaware of the machine-gun fire that was to follow the fire from Heaven.)

'No, the Vatican's hands are by no means clean; nor are Stepinac's. What could he plead in his own defence? The documents condemned him. All he said was, "In all this my conscience is clear." As if we cared about his conscience!

'He got sixteen years. He deserved more. And what was his prison like? He could say Mass in his own chapel. He lived as if at home. He had books and good food. He was fatter when he came out than when he went in. Do you call that prison? After only five years his sentence was remitted — that's to say he was given his freedom on conditions. That was late in 1951. He had the chance to leave the country. In Yugoslavia, the new Yugoslavia, there was no place for him.

'And what did he do? Go to Rome? No, he retired to Krasić, the village where he was born. And there he stays, playing the martyr. Isn't it contemptible? He was offered a safe-conduct to the Italian frontier, and he said, "I'll stay where I am." 'What a saint!'

'And the Vatican has the nerve to make a wretch like that Cardinal. Can you imagine a greater insult to Yugoslavia? A traitor to his country made cardinal! Do you wonder we broke off diplomatic relations with the Vatican? Has Sweden a minister there? And why was there less fuss made in the Italian press when the United States broke off diplomatic relations with the Vatican in 1951? Because

Italy needs dollars and not dinars; because Italy is not after colonies in the States but in the Balkans.'

The springs creaked and the smell of scorched rubber wafted through the car. Zeljko Brihta had talked himself hot.

'This campaign against us shows more clearly than anything that the Vatican is a tool in the hands of imperialist Italy — that Stepinac is a tool in the hands of the Pope.

'Italy must expand.

'Look at Abyssinia. Do you remember how the Pope invoked God's blessing on Mussolini's troops? We haven't forgotten.

'Look at that disastrous Libyan adventure.

'Look at the expedition against the Balkans. Was that the work of a single man, or was it a whole nation trying to sublimate its complexes? At that time the cry was "Dalmatia for Italy!" Now it's "Trieste for Italy!" The next will be "Istria for Italy!" and after that "Dalmatia for Italy!" again.

'Can we put up with this sort of thing? Why should we be Italy's punch-ball?

'What's the good of all these solemn assurances: "No more war between our two countries"? Or the excuses: "Mussolini was a mistake." In the next breath all these fair words and promises are forgotten. Experience has taught us that Italy says one thing in the north and another in the south. We have a good memory, and we don't mean to be tricked.

'What do you think about the Pope? Do you think he's fool enough not to see that Italy's trying to grab territory in the east? Does he imagine we're to be taken in by shocked cries of: "Politics? Politics are not for us!"? If he sees a chance to gather another sheep into his fold, will he let it slip by? Century after century history has shown us that the Vatican always mixes politics with religion. Why should Pius XII be an exception?'

Zeljko Brihta shook his head, flapping his bat's ears.

'They say we don't give our people religious freedom. That's a lie.

We've simply done what must be done in every modern nation: we've separated Church and State.

'I say again: anyone in this country can practise the religion of his choice. It's true, of course, that Communism with its materialistic view of life is not in sympathy with faith in a Christian God, or in other spiritual power. But we don't forbid anyone to hold whatever religious views his conscience bids him. Perhaps we regard religious faith as a relic, as the skeletal remains of dead and unenlightened stages of culture; but we allow our people the freedom to retain it. With us, the Moslems of Bosnia, the Orthodox of Serbia and the Croatian Catholics are as free in their faiths as Jews, atheists and deists. But one thing we will not have; we will not have the Church meddling in politics! Religion is one thing, politics another. The Church is one thing, the State another. The two mustn't be mixed. We get the best co-operation from Orthodox and Moslems: they keep within religious bounds. But the Catholic Church interferes in politics and in the struggle for temporal power. That we will not put up with. And therefore we will not put up with Pius XII. Let him look after his Church, and we'll look after Yugoslavia. We offer freedom of conscience and freedom of religion, but the Catholic Church abuses this freedom, backs up warmongers in exchange for their support and their help in spreading Catholicism at the expense of religious freedom. It's not Yugoslavia that's intolerant, nor Tito, but the Catholic Church. The Vatican is the modern Trojan Horse, loaded with imperialist weapons. Stepinac is the tail of the horse: intolerant, fanatical and not afraid of cold steel when it's a question of sending a soul to God.'

The car coughed. We were only five miles from Krasić. The driver dragged the steering-wheel round, and unwillingly the road-wheels wrenched themselves to the right. We were turning down a by-road. Mud splashed up in a black bow-wave, the car bounded and the springs groaned. Ahead of us appeared a village and above the village a white church steeple. Beyond, the hills were white. Krasić.

A police-guard signed to us to stop. Were our papers in order?

Identity-cards? Passport? Right. But our permit to enter the village
— where was that?

'Haven't they rung through from Zagreb?'

'No.'

Zeljko Brihta:

'I don't understand it. Is there a telephone anywhere?'

'Not here. At the gendarmerie on the main road.'

The driver reversed and turned and ploughed back through the
mire. From the gendarmerie we got on to Zagreb: 'Yes, it's all fixed.'
With a policeman on the running-board we turned once more down
the side-road to Krasić. The sun was shining. The first sunny day for
years, said the policeman. On two flat tyres we entered the village
where a cardinal sat thumbing his Bible. Coarse, fat women balanced
washing on their heads, fat sows rootled round the corners of the
houses, and geese scattered with flapping wings, less from fear of our
horn than of our clattering mudguards. We parked the car on the
slope leading to the church. Behind the church on the further side
of a muddy yard, where a cat and a dog were playing among the
puddles, stood a powder-white, two-storeyed house with a green
door, green shutters and a green roof. An old woman whose hair was
covered by a white veil came limping out. Zeljko Brihta looked at her
coldly. I took her hand; she bobbed and I bowed.

'Is the Cardinal at home, I wonder?'

Cardinal Alojzije Stepinac was sitting a little limply on his sofa, in a
black Dominican gown with thin red piping. A heavy gold cross lay
on his breast. A red skull-cap was pressed down over the tonsure and
the smooth hair, which was untouched by grey. The face was not
that of an elderly man; there were no sharp outlines, no straining of
the skin over the cheek-bones. All the lines were soft, free of any
trace of struggle, yet resolute and firm. They spoke not of conflict but
of an inner peace, won by treaty with higher powers.

The Cardinal did not live in his own house but in that of the young
priest of Krasić, Josip Vraneković. But Father Josip was away that

day. Though it was noon, the room was full of a scented dusk. One little window faced east.

'Yes, this is my prison,' said Cardinal Stepinac. His voice was smooth as catskin; his lips as thin as thread.

We spoke of his health. He had been operated upon a month before.

'My operating theatre was the room next door. I could have gone to Zagreb, of course. But for that I need a permit; and for a permit I have to write a good many letters, and nowadays I write very few. A professor, a great friend of mine, came here from Zagreb and opened me up.'

I asked him about his treatment in prison.

'I've no complaint. The food was good. And I had a small room, like this one, only it had a heavy grille.' The Cardinal raised a finger towards the window. 'There was a chapel too, where I could say Mass. But prison is always prison. Even the village of my childhood has been enclosed by invisible walls. Yes, until Yugoslavia is free, the whole country must be my prison. . . .' He went over to the window and looked out. Grey snow lay in wet drifts over the ground. 'My father was a peasant here, a simple peasant. I used to play here. Now I sit here with my little library — all I own in this world. I read my books and I'm allowed to celebrate Mass every day in the church. I talk to the peasants. They're good, hardworking people, these people of Krasić.'

The Cardinal spoke of Sweden.

'It's a free country, isn't it? Protestant of course, but free. I've heard that a wave of Catholicism is passing over it.' (The Cardinal was plunging down into a more congenial period of history.) 'You've given us so much. St Bridget — a great woman. One of the greatest of our saints.

'Those *Revelations* of hers! They were indeed revelations to me. And Catherine, her daughter — I hope she's not too greatly under-valued among you? And Queen Christina — what a woman that was!

58

'I remember in the twenties, when I was studying at the Germanicum in Rome, there was a Swede, a count, who used to come to the church every Sunday to hear the liturgy. And to think I've forgotten his name. An unusually distinguished and cultured man. He brought his friends to church, first one and then another until at last there was quite a little Swedish colony at Mass.

'I get letters now from all over the world. Everyone is sympathetic — but for myself, I never write now-a-days.'

The Cardinal was thinking of the five diaries which were taken from him in 1946 and which became one of the chief items of documentary evidence in the trial of war-criminals.

'No memoirs either?'

'No, I haven't written anything for seven years. In the old days I used to write a great deal; for instance — '

The conversation slid away from this awkward topic.

'But is there any foundation for all the accusations?'

The Cardinal made no reply, and merely smiled.

'The Glina massacre, for instance – the Serbs who were butchered in front of the altars – baptism at the rifle's point. . . .'

Without altering the tone of his voice, Cardinal Stepinac said, 'We can readily take the blame for that.'

Then followed the phrase which had become a joke all over Yugoslavia; the phrase with which as archbishop he had sought to exculpate himself during the trial of 1946:

'My conscience is clear.'

But when I asked whether or not it was true that the Catholic Church used the Cross to further political aims, the Cardinal smacked his hand down on the table and cried,

'That's a fable and nothing but a fable! A lie — an absurd lie!'

Some inner pressure was released through the escape valve of speech as he continued vehemently:

'A time will come when the truth shall be revealed: the truth of how I tried to save and did save thousands upon thousands of lives. As for the massacres in the churches — what could I do? I'm no politician. Oh, we were lied about – slandered in the vilest way – persecuted with the basest methods. Have they really been able to convince you that religious freedom exists in Yugoslavia? If I were able to, I would tell you of many ways by which the Church and the souls of the people are trampled underfoot. But unfortunately I cannot speak freely; it would merely cause suffering and torture to innocent people.'

Once more the Cardinal sat limp and round-shouldered, fingering the crucifix on the purple-black gown. A narrow ray of sunlight struck a flash from the cross.

'I can see you want to ask why I don't go to Rome, since the frontier's open. Well, if I did, the same thing would happen as happened to my secretary: the gates of Yugoslavia would be locked behind me. That's why I stay and fulfil my task. My place is in Yugoslavia, not the Vatican.'

But as I sat before the Cardinal I thought of Tito's words when in Paris, in 1938, he was reconstructing the disintegrating Communist Party of Yugoslavia: 'Firstly, the Central Committee must be in Yugoslavia and work among the people. One can't expect the workers' struggle for democracy to succeed if their leaders are far from the battlefield. That is a primary condition for victory. To await instructions from outside, to use someone else's head instead of one's own, is a mortal danger for every such movement. A man living outside his country, in exile, degenerates. Better that he should be in his homeland among his own people, fighting side by side with them, sharing with them the good and the bad – even though his life be constantly in danger – than that he should go abroad, far from the movement, far from the people.'

Tito has never been remarkable for taciturnity, but Alojzije Stepinac was silent. By a thin smile he indicated that he was tired, and that as far as he was concerned the conversation had ended with these words: 'I shall stay here. Here among my people, even if it means dying in Krasić.'

Cardinal Alojzije Stepinac, sentenced to sixteen years' imprisonment as a war-criminal, might today have been sitting beside the Papal Throne; he might have wandered in the gardens of the Vatican and looked down upon the city of St Peter. All this he renounced. I knew that Zeljko Brihta, drumming on the table in the hall, would spew up all his contempt: 'A fine martyr!' But the Cardinal's purpose was a deeper one. If he had availed himself of the safe-conduct, the affair would soon have been hushed up, and Tito would have been proclaimed an honest Sancho Panza of tolerance. But Stepinac himself would have become a cardinal among cardinals. He remained where he was, to arouse a storm from the West against the Communist régime. He had become a symbol of the Church under oppression.

At the same time the sweet pain of the martyr's crown of thorns must have had its appeal for Stepinac, as for every true Catholic. Hope beckoned: the hope that one day that crown of thorns would be exchanged for the nimbus of the saint.

Yet what above all else led Stepinac to choose imprisonment in Krasić was not the will to preserve Yugoslavia for Catholicism, nor the lure of becoming St Alojzije. Another man could have done his work, and to invest in a halo was but a doubtful speculation. His motives lay deeper than that. They lay in his private reckoning with his judges. Why had he declared that he took the blame upon himself? Because he regarded this blame as fictitious. It was the fruit not of his actions but of the accusations made by anti-Catholic Communists. So long as his judges would not exonerate him from the crimes they laid upon him, so long did he wish the guilt of them to rest upon his shoulders. In accepting their favour he would be acknowledging the crime. It was a logical idea, for what would have become of Christianity if Christ had begged himself down off the cross and gone his way as a pardoned conjuror? For Stepinac there was but one solution: to be the Cardinal who will die in Krasić — to remain a criminal in the eyes of the Communists. Willingly he bore the blame laid upon him. He did not want a freedom the acceptance of which would imply an admission of real guilt.

Tito had not reasoned so far. He had been foolish enough to make a superfluous gesture towards the West, not reckoning with the fact that Stepinac must be a criminal in order to save his soul.

When I returned to Zagreb, a friend of mine, Dr G—, was waiting for me in the Gradska Kavana. With my thoughts still full of Stepinac I led the conversation round to him.

'It's a complicated affair; far, far more complicated than you might think. When the Nazis came in 1941, Stepinac met an ideology which, like that of Communism, was emphatically anti-Catholic. But the Ustaša – the Yugoslav fascist party – differed from irrational, heathen Nazism in questions of religion, and was openly Pope-minded. In the war against anti-Catholic Nazism, Stepinac chose a power which would support him and the Vatican, but in so doing he chose to be – from the point of view of the People's Front and the Communists – a traitor to his country and a war-criminal.

'One can never absolve Stepinac from having known about the atrocities committed in Yugoslavia during Pavelić's reign of terror. In his eagerness to convert the Greek-Orthodox Serbs he made use of the Ustaša. He states in a report to the Pope that 300,000 became converts, yet he had to make the journey to Rome to relieve his agony of soul after the massacres of the Serbs. It would be wrong, though, to say that Stepinac did not work for a more conciliatory policy. In the cathedral itself he preached several sermons which in veiled phrases criticized the methods of government by force. Unfortunately the action that Stepinac took to save lives he took chiefly as a private individual — as Pavelić's friend. He never came forward openly, like Bishop Berggrav in Norway — and this was a weakness bordering on the criminal.

'It's also untrue to say that the Vatican supported Pavelić. It was impossible for Fascist Croatia to obtain true diplomatic representation with the Pope, since as long as war continued the Vatican never officially formed fresh diplomatic ties. But in a practical sense the co-operation between the Ustaša and the Pope was good, and in many letters to the Vatican, members of the Ustaša league were mentioned as being good Catholics.'

But the Cardinal stays in his little village where everything is as it was when he stood dreaming there in his clogs, on a day like today, watching other children play and not able to play with them; looking at the mountains pressing snow-white against the horizon; feeling that he would be more at home beyond them.

When I took my leave of Stepinac, I left a cardinal who had chosen personal victory. He limped out into the muddy yard in front of the house and said goodbye. I didn't know then that I was the last who would be allowed to visit him. After I left, a wall of police was set up round the village.

Pigs were rootling in the garbage. Hens flapped along the walls of the houses. A pensioned padre from the neighbouring parish, Josip Simečki, took me into the church where every Sunday the Cardinal celebrated Mass. Zeljko Brihta, who had been waiting on the ground floor of Vraneković's house, came too, walking at a little distance. It was a strange procession that passed through the church that winter day in Krasić: an atheist, a Communist, a driver and a retired Catholic priest. In the house alongside a cardinal sat and looked out through the window.

When we came out of the church into the pale light of a January sun, five geese were patrolling the muddy road. But that road did not lead to Rome.

6. SQUARE OF THE REPUBLIC

IN the ice of the Zagreb night the Square of the Republic lay like a deserted football-ground of cement. No cars threw their lights down the Ilica, the main street. No trams clanged their bells; no neon-lights blended their colours with the purple-black night. No snow covered the square, but the lily-of-the-valley street-lamps shed light about their stems. A few night strollers had petrified into pigeons and frozen fast in the feeble radiance. Their words died in the darkness between lamps. Fixed beneath these lamps, the upside-down soup-plates of the loudspeakers were empty and silent. It was Sunday. Or Monday, or Tuesday.

At a refreshment-room in a narrow street, some blocks from the Square of the Republic, a student lies dying . . .

The Cathedral where Stepinac preached thrust its nineteenth-century Gothic spires into the sky. From the blue-grey air seeped a streak of blood-red. At dawn the square awoke. Sunshine climbed slowly up the steps to the market-place behind the Square of the Republic; cocks crowed cheerfully on their last morning. Women from the outlying villages carried baskets on their heads. Women from the villages wore slippers in the cold, and coarse thick stockings. The newly-awakened sun surveyed their colourful skirts and white aprons drowsily. The women from the villages had a patina born of wind and soil and rain, and they carried onions in broad necklaces round their necks. They squatted on the ground, with their baskets of eggs before them.

The dying student has had his head bashed in by a chair. He can hear a distant moaning and feels something cold, wet and black over his temples. Those standing round him — the bar-boys, and Pavle, Miro and Pero, melt away in the mist.

64

The Gardener of Hvar looks across the water from Spanjola Fortress.

Onofrio de la Cava's Fountain. Beyond it the Placa leads past the Franciscan Church towards the city gate and Ploče, the Paradise Lost of the Dubrovnik millionaires.

Diagonally below the steps the policeman stood directing the non-existent traffic and waiting for a time that is to come. Diagonally across the square the shoeblacks clattered their boards and tucked their toes into huge shoes with four-inch-thick wooden soles. A car glided along the row of houses on the other side of the Hotel Dubrovnik, hooting full blast — the herald of an age of motorized brutality. Trams, blue and rusty, dirty and squealing, were heroes still unconquered.

These, then, are the remains of the brawl, and its causes were very trivial: a student pulled a waiter's nose because he thought the fellow was being too long in bringing the beer. Good Lord, is that anything to fight about, in a tavern?

But about the big cafés – about the Kavana of the Hotel Dubrovnik, and the Gradska Kavana, the City Café – there lingered a breath of Austria-Hungary, though they had been built long after that time. They are, as I said, marvellous theatres, with stalls and balconies, and orchestras that play from a platform between the balconies: the Harry Lime theme in waltz-time and The Blue Danube as a foxtrot.

The girl with the platter of cakes wandered among the tables; and nowhere in Yugoslavia are there such cakes and pastries as in Zagreb. Nowhere such steaming coffee with cream foaming over the edge like an exploding atom-bomb. But the tea, even in the Gradska Kavana, is as wishy-washy as in all the other towns. View across the tables: crossword puzzlers, newspaper-readers and fat ladies with fat slices of cake.

It was they who began it; it was their fault, thinks the waiter who had seized the chair and hit out with it. And the other waiters, those who had hastened to the aid of the nose-pulled slayer, say, 'It wasn't your fault, comrade — it was they who picked the quarrel.' But the student lies dying on the floor.

The sheet of frost over the big windows overlooking the Square of the Republic melted to a wet mist. Wipe the pane, wipe one's hand and look out. Miroslav Krleža writes in his novel *The Return of Filip Latinović:* 'There sits Filip in the coffee-house watching the people as they pass by in the street, and reflecting how strange and mysterious

65

this eternal movement is. People go past, bearing in their musty entrails boiled chickens' heads, the sorrowful eyes of birds, the joints of oxen, the legs of horses; and last night these creatures gaily wagged their tails and the hens cackled in their runs on the eve of their death. But now all has ended in human viscera; and this transformation, this guzzling, is in a word: life in the cities of Western Europe in the shadow of Western civilization.'

But the student dies, and at the trial the waiter is acquitted, because it was in self-defence that he happened to kill and because it was the student who started the fight.

Opposite the Hotel Dubrovnik on the other side of the square gleamed a row of tall windows: The Authors' Society. Through those rooms moved the men of the pen: Miroslav Krleža himself, the pioneer, the admired and unattainable. But there was also the genial bull-dog Angelinović, the secretary of the society, who for two years had been wrestling with the translation of *Orlando Furioso* and who was already lauded to the skies for his rendering of Shakespeare's sonnets. The writer of socialist short stories, Simić, wore his hat at an elegant angle, but the poet Cesarić carried the riddle of the sphinx in his face, and it is thus that Kosta Angeli Radovani has sculptured him. 'But suppose you wanted to criticize the socialist system? Suppose you wrote that Marxism is lies – long live the capitalist state – could such a book be printed?' Simić burst out furiously: 'But that's a lie! How can literature which is not true be good literature?'

A year later a man steps into the little dive in the back street behind the Square of the Republic, and orders a glass of wine. What could be more natural?

How many squares have a place in our conscience: the Piazzetta of Venice, Djama el Fna, Puerta del Sol, Piazza Navona with its fountain of the rivers of the world, the Place des Contrescarpes of the oysters, Piccadilly Circus — but evening was coming on, and every evening the loudspeakers poured out their strident contents over the Square of the Republic. Folk-dances broke out thunderously in the echo of the last sentence of the news-broadcast — but no one dances in the Square of the Republic. A white screen was unrolled down the façade of the Authors' Society building, and a film-projector stretched its arm of light across the square. For an hour the Square of the Republic was transformed into a giant cinema. On the screen appeared first Kalle Anka, but then a vast hydro-electric installation, an electrical engineering-works and a Yugoslav woman parachutist. But over and over again came the classic 'Conference-scene': a man talking — a hall packed with bearded men and sturdy women — the speaker — behind him, above Tito's portrait, the Yugoslavian banners — the peroration — applauding hands. Heavy snowflakes sank down through the cold.

Nothing could be more natural if the man had simply emptied his wine-glass and gone out. This man has been here several evenings lately. Just for a glass of wine, thinks the waiter who killed the student.

But there are squares with other names: Love Square, Pain Square and the Square of Loss. And every one of them owns the people who look down from their windows and count the pigeons on the paving below. And the same square can be for one that of Flight, for another of Remaining. There are the squares of Happiness and of Terror — but this was the Square of the Republic in Zagreb. At twelve o'clock the salvoes of big guns crashed upon the roofs and at each salute the pigeons bent their pain in a bow against the sky. Yugoslavia had a president, Marshal Tito. Above the Authors' Society building blazed a blue neon sign: *Živio Tito!* Long Live Tito! And in the shop-windows all round the square his portrait was embedded in flowers. The Square of the Republic, the square of shabby coats. A man was speaking from the balcony of the Authors' Society.

The waiter puts the glass down on the table with a friendly smile ('This man will soon be one of our regulars') and steps back. But the customer pulls out a revolver and with three shots at the heart rounds off the waiter's life. Then he quietly empties his glass and awaits the police.

From my place on the other side of the square the speaker looked small and insignificant. I could catch a few words: President — Com-

67

munist — Socialist — the Vatican — Ustaša — Massed voices filled the air: '*Živio Tito! Živio Tito!*'

'*Why did you kill him?*' *asks the police-constable.*

'*Why? Why? What would you have done if you'd been the student's father?*'

The man on the balcony spoke from out of a maw of darkness. 'President — Communist — the Vatican — Ustaša — Yugoslavia —' Behind, the windows were bright. A hurricane arose over the Square of the Republic: '*Živio Tito! Živio Tito!*' But when I looked about me people were standing silent and still. Only the loudspeakers were yelling. That night I left the Square of the Republic and took the train back to Rijeka. The Square of the Republic lay as deserted as a cement football-ground on a January night.

PART II

7. THE SIX PILLARS OF DIOCLETIAN

THE sooty white steam-boat of barely a thousand tons hooted farewell to Rijeka. Night still lay heavy over the harbour. Six clock-strokes bounced off the quays and the lanterns on the jetty were short of breath.

Then light began to filter down over the Adriatic. The waves changed their colour from lilac to grey, from grey to blue. The horizon swallowed Rijeka, the dockyards of Rijeka, the prostitutes' hopes of American seamen, and the trolleybus line that Rijeka inherited from Italy. And Marija — where was Marija — ?

Two winds rule the Adriatic: the *jugo* of summer, and the *bora*. The luke-warm, persistent south wind and the wind from the north which, cold and capricious, hurtles down from the hills.

For an hour there were heavy seas — and this at dawn, when sea-sick people are more mucous than at any other hour of the day. The boat was called the *Kotor* and she wrestled with the seas. Water foamed in through the scuttles of the third-class passengers' quarters: a little box forward, on the upper deck. And the Yugoslav chief engineer on leave was as green as algae, and spat.

'Struth, she rolls worse than any tub I know.'

Then he did as the rest of us did: vanished in search of a lee side. But the *bora* twists like a corkscrew and there was no shelter anywhere.

Suddenly we seemed to be sucked forward as if someone were pulling at a lever; there was a jerk and a swirl — and serenely as a duck the *Kotor* was gliding through the Dalmatian archipelago. Breakfast, that had been hovering luke-warm and greasy in one's throat, slipped down and settled again. The sun unrolled its blanket of light and turned the Adriatic into a warm bed in January.

71

This archipelago is a very different thing from our Swedish one: bleak and stony indeed, but not defiant or arrogant — not an army in constant battle with the water. It is soft and yellow and as it were baked in sand. It is smooth and gentle, like the humps of buried camels rising from a sea of blue sand.

The island of Pag was a streak drawn by a sun-pencil on the water. Miles separated the clusters of white cubes – five or six – which were the villages. An affinity exists between houses and cypresses and pine-clad hillocks. Cézanne could have cut rectangles out of this low coast. Behind the island rose the Velebit Mountains, burdened with pure blue snow, and above them the sky was like a colour-film.

This coast is the coast of Venice. For nearly four hundred years, up to the time of the Napoleonic wars, the Doge hid Dalmatia beneath the hem of his mantle. Every town along the coast as far as Dubrovnik is a little Venice, with its own Piazza San Marco, its own Piazzetta. Rab on the island of Rab; Zadar, not yet arisen from its ruins, which Miroslav Krleža dreamed of turning into a Yugoslav Socialist Cambridge; Šibenik, whose lights panted feebly in the water. For by now the sun had packed its trunk and left for other seas.

Split, the capital of Dalmatia, sprang out of nothing and mirrored its lights with vanity in the water.

Dalmatia shivered in its winter night. Spring, which had smiled for a few hours of the day, stiffened to a frozen grimace. It is true that no snow had fallen on this coast for fifty years, but its nights were blue-lipped, with aching finger-joints. Here on the coast of palms, where summer reigns for two-thirds of the year, and the dream of summer for the remaining third, winter nights are a nightmare of shuddering cold. Cafés without fires, hotel-rooms without heaters.

My window faced the end wall of a house, mildewed with damp. When I breathed out I breathed a cloud. I slept huddled in my sleeping-bag between blankets and sheets, and a dank chill seeped through the proofing of the bag. Mornings were horrors of dingy, shivering grey; but when I came out on to the open space before the Hotel

Central, the miniature Town Hall in late Gothic style was dazzling white in the sun.

The hours of sunshine in the middle of the day felt like a Judas kiss; yet while the kiss lasted the memory of the night's cold was lightly, thoughtlessly banished.

Split. Palm-trees, blue sea, the colours of a picture-postcard. Along the water's edge ran a *promenade anglaise*. One of Yugoslavia's seven or eight motor-ships entered the harbour stern-first and her wash lapped gently against the promenade. On this, the Titova Obala – Tito's Beach Road – were shoeblacks, rags, the blue coats and black pistol-holsters of the military police, porters with clattering hand-carts. Nowhere in Yugoslavia had poverty so naked a skin as beneath these palm-trees; not even in Macedonia or along the Albanian border. Perhaps it was shown up by the mercilessly revealing light. Perhaps it was because this poverty was like the poverty of Naples: dirty, paralysing, humiliating. Those ragged heaps of resignation waiting in the market-place had nothing of the proud, embattled poverty which makes the Serbs such heroic figures. This was Italy's legacy: a dire and degrading legacy to set against that of renaissance cathedrals, campaniles and graceful balustrades.

But on the other side of the promenade marched a wall of grey houses, with antique columns embodied in the façade.

'Now, now!' yelled the bus-driver. 'Easy does it!'

But it was just a matter of elbows; the bus was elastic. The garage dazzled white and hurt one's eyes in the January sun. The gravelled space in front of it sent up a vicious cloud of dust; it was like a photograph of Morocco.

'Now then — what do you think this is? A sardine-tin?'

Curses flew like blows, There, a flower-pot was smashed. 'Mind my eggs — for Christ's sake mind my eggs!' The bus jerked forward with us all higgledy-piggledy, and somehow by the mercy of Providence we were rattling alongside the blue water, six dusty kilometres to Salona. The bus skidded along the gravel.

'Solin! Solin!'

Solin – which is Croat for Salona – on a lappet of the Adriatic, is two things. There is the living village of Solin, which is the dead, dried-up, old crones' village. And there is the capital of the Roman province of Dalmatia, the dead city of Salona, which, is the living one; it has survived Latins and barbarians and is, after Pompeii and Herculaneum, the best preserved of all ruined Roman cities.

And I was looking for ruins. Peasants dug in their gardens and a bush stretched its flowering boughs across the road. The road ran through ruins — not classical ruins, but gutted houses, monuments to guerrilla battles; roofless, with no glass in the windows. A path from the road led up towards a greyish-white belt of vineyards, mounting in shallow steps to the sky. The path was narrow and full of potholes. Towards me came a boy driving a white ox, and I jumped into a ditch to make way, stumbling over something hard. A Corinthian capital lay at my feet; I was standing within the walls of an excavated house.

Higher up I touched a stony, twisting stem of acanthus, feeling slightly giddy. Looking out across the cautiously-sloping roofs, the colonnades, atrium by atrium, I saw men in togas and sandals conversing in the violet shadow of the houses — women with water-jars on their heads gliding cat-like through the alleyways. What's the name of the boy drilling his playfellows?

'That's Caius Aurelius Valerianus; he's the son of a slave in Dioclea. Something about that boy tells me he'll go far. . . . But if you'll come up the hill with me I will show you what was born of that lad's iron will.'

My companion leads me along streets and through houses. Time is under a double exposure. The broken columns support blue and red roofs. The walls at one and the same moment have roofs and glower hollowly like skulls. Between giant cactus we climb up on to a road that commands a view of all Salona.

'Look at that stone. The inscription is clear enough for you to read.'

74

I read: COEMETERIUM LEGIS SANCTAE CHRISTIANAE – MARTYRUM SALONITANORUM MANASTRINE.

'You mean —'

'Exactly. He grew into a very powerful man, that little Caius Aurelius Valerianus, and he had the blood of many on his hands. But follow the road between the cypresses; at the end of it is the custodian's house, and on the left you'll find the martyrs' burial-ground. I shall stay here.'

And between the trees of death and coolness I go up to the place where the martyrs of Salona lie in coffins of stone.

The custodian's house guards the Basilica — a skeleton of foundations and snapped-off pillars. In moonlight a romantic place for dreaming of wraiths. The gateway of the custodian's house is embellished by two columns, and above the doorway roars a lion's head. The trellis-work of the garden is supported by pillars stolen from the city below. What a hotch-potch of antiquity!

As my companion bade me I turn left and emerge among the tombs: little houses with broken roofs and ears listening at the four corners. The ancient graveyard of Salona is a chaos of death. Some of the sarcophagi are still sunk in the earth, others are overturned and broken open. Others have holes in the lids as if spirits had forced their way out. Some of the coffins are no bigger than a beheaded child.

'Well,' says my companion on my return through the avenue of death's tall trees; 'Well, are you satisfied with the work of Caius Aurelius Valerianus?'

His voice is lighter, less serene than before, as if it belonged to someone else.

We follow the road leading to the sea, walking silently. A soldier leads his donkey past me, raising his hand: '*Dobar dan!*' Good day. A peasant is watering his horses at a trough of green, sickly water.

'Over there is the Greek theatre; we seldom use it now, and only for trashy plays by Plautus. Sophocles is quite out of fashion. Young people have very different pleasures these days; the times are poisoned by a dreadful frivolity. Do you hear that roaring? Those are the lions to be used at this evening's games. That building is the amphitheatre.'

We go in. The amphitheatre of Salona has an oval arena, and in it an old man is sweeping up last night's refuse: blood and guts.

'I feel cold here,' says my companion. 'But before I say goodbye I'd like you to go with me a little way up the hill, high enough to see as far as Emperor Diocletian's palace. As you'll have realized, that Caius Aurelius Valerianus is none other than Diocletian, the worst-feared emperor of all time, more cruel than either Nero or Caligula. A great man, but terrible in his greatness. It's a hundred years now since he died.'

We climb the hill. My self-appointed cicerone walks lightly as if on winged feet. There are no paths here, only vineyards and olive-groves.

'We're high enough now,' says my companion.

I turn. Three miles to the southward a high building stands on the fringe of the sea. I shade my eyes to see more clearly. Solin, which I passed through a while ago, has sunk into the ground and been covered with fields, but a tall-arched aqueduct leads away and away to the building in the distance.

'That is the palace of Diocletian,' says my companion. 'The biggest in the world. Not even the Pharaohs—'

'Thank you,' I say. 'I've just come from there, and it was a big modern town, with traces in it of Venice.'

'You're joking,' says the man beside me. 'What's Venice? And "big modern town?" You've got it all wrong. Certainly it looks like a town, but it's a palace — the most fantastic palace one could imagine. Diocletian himself is buried in the middle of it, in a very singular mausoleum. If you have good eyesight you can see the Golden Gate through which the road from Salona runs into the palace. And what you think looks small is in fact enormous. The whole palace is en-closed by walls and towers, and there's room in those walls for a strong garrison. As you can see, perhaps, the western side is right on the water. There are steps there. When Diocletian returned to Dalmatia from Rome, he landed at those steps, and later all the envoys from the Senate came there when they wanted advice in affairs of state. For although Diocletian had by then abdicated, yet until his death he was accounted the only true authority in the Empire.'

We sit down on the grass, my cicerone and I, and without noticing an aircraft buzzing overhead he goes on with his tale:

'If you can get leave of the prefecture – as you should be able to, coming from so far away – you really must visit the palace. You can always make the excuse that you want to offer sacrifice to Diocletian. Do you know, my great-great-grandfather was a scribe there, and through him a certain amount about Diocletian's private life has been handed down in our family. It's a pretty old family, as it happens – one of the oldest in Salona – and I can trace my ancestry back to the time when Emperor Augustus brought the city under Roman dominion and made it the capital of all this coast. You can see that it's splendidly situated, for land- and sea-routes to ancient Hellas and the Orient pass this way.

'Try to get into the palace, then. I don't expect you'll be allowed into the Temple of Jupiter or the Emperor's private apartments; but if you're interested in architecture, you must certainly study the peristyle with the tall columns, between the Temple of Jupiter and the mausoleum. Travellers who come here admit that they have never seen any place where such widely contrasting elements unite in such harmonious perfection. Yet every detail and every least ornament was planned and executed with meticulous care. It's even said that this core of Diocletian's palace excels the Forum Romanum itself, for the Forum has – for all its richness and grandeur – the defect of being the product of different periods, different builders and different tastes and styles. But the palace of Diocletian is the creation of one man. By the power of his genius he balanced and interwove the diverse elements, and fused them in a creation of superb beauty.

'You'll be thinking me verbose, magniloquent; but – to my shame I say it – I can never cease to marvel at and praise this triumph of

77

architecture. Yet even the double peristyle is inferior to the mausoleum itself. As you will see, the octagon of the mausoleum is surrounded by an arcade and guarded by a black sphinx which Diocletian brought from Egypt. Nowhere in our part of the world have I seen such buildings; and though the Pantheon in Rome is supposed to be an offspring of the same thought, I firmly believe what my father said he'd heard from my grandfather, who in his turn heard it from his grandfather: namely, that a Syrian merchant brought the plans with him when he visited Diocletian. Diocletian had a great fondness for the East, and would have liked to resemble one of the omnipotent despots that Oriental princes are said to be. He mingled his faith in Jupiter and the other Roman gods with Oriental rites, and I smile to myself sometimes when I reflect that the model for the Emperor's eternal resting-place is borrowed from the region where Christ – whom he so detested – lived and worked. But isn't history full of such ironies?'

As we sit here on the grass, where butterflies flicker among the flowers and bees hum, a sudden tremendous noise breaks out down there in Salona. Bells are rung and the air quivers with the blasts of copper horns. On the broad main street men are mustering, in light armour and plumed helmets. Horses are led forward harnessed to chariots, and soon the whole procession sets forth towards the east. My companion sighs.

'What's happening?' I ask.

'The same old story. The barbarians have invaded and now fresh blood must be sacrificed to hold them back. We're attacked by enemies from all directions. Soon there'll be no young men left in Salona, and that will be the end of our fair city. A proposal has been made by our senior citizens that we should beg admittance to the palace, and take our stand behind its walls. And that may be our only hope. But I shudder to think of the day when all that loveliness will be soiled by our ignorant and unschooled people. "To the Styx with beauty!" is their cry — and how savage are their curses! "What's the good of beauty if we can't live?" '

My companion sighs yet more heavily and plucks a flower from the grass.

'I don't know why you came here,' he says. 'And perhaps I'm taking up too much of your time; but this Diocletian fascinates me, although I ought to hate him.'

'It's often so with dictators,' I remark.

'Anyhow, I should like to tell you what I've heard, so that you won't leave this region quite ignorant of its past. As I said just now. Diocletian was a true Illyrian, the son of a slave. He enlisted in the Roman army and, as so often happens in time of war, he won rapid promotion. He went to Rome and became Praetor, and when Emperor Numerian was murdered he was proclaimed Emperor by the Prefects. This was in the two hundred and eighty-fifth year after the birth of Christ. His first act was symbolic of his whole career. He condemned the Prefect of the Guard Asper, Numerian's slayer, to death and ran him through with his own sword. While seeming to punish a crime – the crime which crowned his own ambitions – he rid himself of his most dangerous rival.

'After this he made a tremendous vow which threw Rome into a frenzy of excitement: he promised to restore the Empire to its former glory. And when that was done he would retire, he said, into private life. A promise at once so challenging and so humble can never have been made by any other Roman. And the strange thing was he kept it. But the methods he used! I'm thinking now of the completely totalitarian state that he created, in which every individual, from the Emperor himself down to the meanest slave, had his rigidly-appointed place. I'm thinking of the re-introduction of the Roman gods and the appalling persecution of the Christians.

'Diocletian settled in Nicomedea near Byzantium, and when his palace there caught fire it was the signal for the massacre of Christians all over the Empire. What an ingenious idea it is to inflame the masses against their enemies by blaming these enemies for some national disaster! Nero had been a master of the art, and you may be sure that the same simple method will be used for the rest of time.

'But as I said, Diocletian succeeded in what he set himself to do, and twenty years after coming to power he abdicated and returned to his native land, which for all of us who were born here is dearer than any other place on earth.

'Various tales have been handed down to us from my great-great-grandfather about life within the palace walls. Dramas were played out there that were never performed in any theatre; intrigues were woven that no author has ever imagined. This palace, you understand, was situated on the very borderline between opposite and irreconcilable extremes: East and West, Christ and Jupiter, Rome and the barbarians who now, since the death of Diocletian, threaten to destroy us. My great-great-grandfather declared too, though I wouldn't stake my toga on the truth of it, that both the Empress and her daughter worshipped – in the strictest secrecy – that "whey-faced Jesus of Nazareth," as Diocletian called him.'

As he is speaking, fresh tumult breaks out below in Salona. Two carts filled with dead or dying men are now being driven into the town and these men are laid out along the shady side of the street. Women and children rush to them and the air is filled with the wildest weeping, groaning, screaming and lamentation.

But butterflies flutter in the grass and bees hum.

'There you can see,' says my invisible companion, 'another sign of how the world is falling to pieces. You have come to us at an unhappy moment in our history; you should have chosen a century or two earlier, when the future was great with promise and when everyone fancied it would bring us a better world; not this world of pain and suffering. Do you hear those roars? Those are the lions from their caves beneath the amphitheatre. In the daytime we mourn our dead and at night we triumph when our slaves are torn to shreds by wild beasts. What sort of people are these I'm living among? The Last Day is approaching, and the whole earth is doomed.'

He rises and shakes his toga. We go down among the vineyards as far as the road above the city, and there my cicerone points to Salona, saying:

View of Dubrovnik Cathedral and the back of the Rectors' Palace.

St Blaise's Church and Orlando with his flagstaff, seen from the street where
Pero Lujak had his fish-restaurant.

'I must return to my city. Perhaps in spite of everything it may one day be immortal. Immortality is our only hope on this earth. . . . If you take the road past the amphitheatre you'll come out on the highway between the palace and Tragurion. While you're in this region you shouldn't fail to see Tragurion, which was the largest Greek city on the coast. If you have the patience to wait, you're sure to get a lift there in some cart or other.'

He gives me his hand in farewell, and as I hold it mine turns quite cold and there's a flickering haze before my eyes, as when one stands up suddenly after lying with one's head down. When I released his hand he was gone, and with him the whole city below me — all the men in their yellow or red togas, the weeping women and the warriors bleeding to death on the shady side of the main street. The lions had ceased their roaring, but a donkey jeered behind the amphitheatre. And before my eyes the theatre divided as if under an invisible scalpel, and section after section was laid bare. The man who had been sweeping sand over patches of blood now had a rake in his hand and was clearing the weeds from his kitchen-plot in the middle of the arena. Past and present had grown together and with my present dizziness I could not keep the epochs apart. Two oil-storage tanks – silver blocks belonging to Jugonafta – rose on the opposite side of the high road.

But there came the rattle of a cart, such as my companion had spoken of; and while I debated whether to hail it or not, it stopped. Then I saw that it was a bus – the bus to Šibenik – and a face I seemed to recognize grinned through the glassless window of the driver's cab:

'Well, have you taken root, or are you coming?'

So I arrived at the Tragurion of the Greeks, though for me it had become the Dalmatian Trogir. I crossed a bridge and came into the little square with its loggia and the famous mediaeval cathedral of San Nikola; it was as dark and shut as a refrigerator. Heavy shadow lay over Radovan's doorway, where Adam stood, ugly and ashamed. Eve was a worn-out woman with sagging breasts.

Through a narrow street I crossed the island which supports Trogir and passed over a new bridge to Ciovo, Trogir's island neighbour. Short-necked palms swaggered above the water. The Carmelite tower to the north thrust up its menacing silhouette. The narrow sound, the row of houses along the quay, the palms, the bridge and the people on it, the bay towards Split softer than blue cotton-wool, isles, boys in boats, fishing-craft, workmen returning from a factory, the sun diving into the sea — this was tranquillity.

I desired no change.

Let everything be itself. Involved and complex thoughts died in the sunset.

No more exquisite punishment could have been devised for Adam and Eve. Let those who desecrate such a Paradise by biting the abstract apple of knowledge be carved in stone in front of a cathedral, with the ever-frozen shadow of the square upon them.

The peace that filled me was like the note of the smallest bell in a campanile.

Not until the sun was utterly drowned did I return to the square with its cathedral and step into the old Town Hall of Trogir, which is now Uzljebrka Boso's inn. In the courtyard the builder's name is carved in stone: Matteus Gosković 1645.

There I drank wine and waited for the bus back to Split.

In the half-dreams of the bus-ride Salona returned: the final devastating assault of the Slavs, the flight, the last stand behind the walls of Diocletian's palace. The new town beginning to grow within the palace. The demolition of the mausoleum. The vengeance of the Christians, the desecration of the corpses, the conversion of the burial-chamber to a church. And this was another of history's pranks: by its transformation into a Christian temple the mausoleum of Anti-Christ was rescued from decay. Yet another stroke of irony: this heathen temple erected in the era of the basilicas was the forerunner of San Marco in Venice five hundred years later, and the idea of the centralized church. Culture is a chain of paradoxes.

82

On this night, which was bright with moonlight, I passed for the first time through the gateway which was once the Golden Gate to Salona, and entered the maze of alleys on the foundations of the imperial palace. The six free Corinthian columns of the peristyle stood slender, tall, liberated, in the moonlight.

Time after time I returned to these columns, to the heart of the palace. I stayed in Split for a week, merely to be able to come back to this. In the pale rays of the morning sun, in the revealing light of midday, in the shadowplay of afternoon and in the rose of twilight; but above all in this moonlight, which breathed life into the stone.

All else in the city seemed to me worthless, and I forget the name of the square in front of the Hotel Bellevue; and yet this square, despite its all too obvious mimicry of the Piazza in Venice, was perhaps the most perfect of its kind of all the Dalmatian coast.

How could I have time for it, when I had to listen to Diocletian's columns? Pillars have tongues, too.

The massive Doric columns of the temple of Paestum boasted of the weight they could carry, and showed off their muscles above the patches of snow. The six free pillars of Diocletian's peristyle on the eastern side (and the six on the west which have been filled in by the walls of houses) have never borne a roof. They stood there in their glory, almost without purpose. But the light structure above, the architrave, saved them from being solely decorative. It was the mighty conception of the architect that those columns carried; but instead of parading their strength they sought to show how lightly and effortlessly they bore their burden. Like hinds, if hinds were columns.

I sat at their foot and watched the children playing in the shadow of the peristyle. The shadow lay like a gate across the open square.

Someone has said that architecture is frozen music. Then is music liberated architecture? If these six pillars were dissolved in music, what transcendently pure and lofty notes would be born! The men who shaped those columns – were they seeking to embody the rapturous theme of man's freedom – were they instilling into stone the dream of hind and bird? And had the Doric columns been made by men chained horribly, ineluctably, to their destiny? With all its might, all its muscular strength, the Doric column cannot free itself from the weight it is condemned to bear. An Oedipus story in marble.

But what a queer contradiction: the compressed Doric column dates from a time when humanity was approaching what was perhaps its peak — when spirit and matter were closer to one another than at any time since; whereas the liberated peristyle rose at the one moment in all those centuries when defeat was a fact, and the incongruities that had till then been unified were drifting further and further apart until the rift was final.

This palace has fascinated generations of scholars: Spon and Whiler, Cassa and Lavallée, Niemann, Herbard — famous archaeologists who have assembled the remains of Diocletian's work and set up their reconstructions in archaeological museums. Foremost of them all, perhaps, is the Scots architect Robert Adam who came here at the end of the eighteenth century to engrave his *Ruins of the Palace of the Emperor Diocletian at Spalato in Dalmatia*.

I stayed here for a week and was able to abstract from my mind the image of the Venetian campanile by the mausoleum. I saw children playing between the free-standing columns, and windows being thrown open between those that were now in the wall. Washing was hoisted in those windows. And when I tired of looking at the children and of being looked at, I dubbed one of them my knight with a toffee; he drove away the rest and together we went down to the palms and the water, to Obala Titova, the *promenade anglaise* of the shoeblacks. The sun was setting. the fishing-boats had chugged away and the motor-ship glided like a burning torch from the harbour.

8. THE STORY OF THE CATS OF HVAR

HVAR is the city of cats.
They sleep under the palms, they steal among the petti-coats of the jar-carrying women, they balance on the walls and they are the terror of the cathedral rats.

Hvar is the city of cats.

When Athens was the centre of the world and Hvar was called Pharos, wild cats hunted young birds in the crevices of the rocks. A cat still lies in the shade of the Greek urns which the sea gave back to Hvar and which lean against the wall of the Franciscan refectory.

A flock of angry cats hissed at the Roman dignitaries as their creaking galleys pulled in to the island, on the way to Emperor Diocletian's new palace outside Salona.

Rome fell and Hvar acquired a Croat king. (Post-revolutionary historians are very careful to point this out.) But the cats were just as grey at dusk, just as smooth and elusive, just as savage and fiery.

For three hundred years Hungarians, Venetians and Turks fought over this island. But the cats were stronger than they.

From the heights behind Hvar – from the southern mountain and the higher one in the north, between which runs the valley road to Starigrad on the other side of the island – cats watched the building of the thirteenth century cathedral and bared their teeth at the bishop who was installed there.

When the plague fetched dead men from every house the cats survived; they survived the Doge by the Lagoon and his four centuries of unbounded, dazzling power.

They were there when the French took Spanjola, the white fort on the northern hill, and built on the southern one their fire-breathing dragon Napoleone. On his first night there the commandant could not sleep for the frightful miaowing outside his window. The second night was the same, and at a quarter past two he roared to the servant sleeping outside his door.

'For God's sake kill that damned cat!'

But the servant returned from the moonlight saying:

'Sir, that devil-cat is everywhere, but I'm not the man to catch it. Yet, sir, I fought at Austerlitz.'

Today three dusty soldiers and a thirsty pack-ass were struggling up the zig-zag track to the fort.

An old speckly-yellow cat was taking his morning stroll through Hvar. He had padded down from the terraces by Spanjola and now glided through steep, crooked streets. Past Gradska Loža – the Town Loggia – which Michele Sanmicheli of Verona built for Hvar in 1516, and out into the square. Outside the Loggia hung a poster: *Veliki ples!* Grand Ball. And the yellow-speckled cat which was also a cat in a bad temper hissed and bristled. He went down to the edge of the quay to see whether there was a fishing-boat in to beg a herring from. Yes, over there by the north quay rocked a grey, two-masted herring-boat.

The cat stretched himself and skipped along the line of houses – the post-office, the harbour-tavern and the bookseller's – and went over to the boat. But what was this? A tiny little soldier with a red star in his cap and a loaded rifle was patrolling the quay. Miaow, said the cat, feeling degraded at having to beg. But the soldier kicked out and the cat darted up among the cactuses on the other side. Aha, he thought; nothing doing here. In the stern of the boat six fishermen sat gazing glumly at their gear, which had been put ashore. *La Vittoria* was the name painted on the vessel's counter, and she was the twenty-fifth Italian boat in two years to be held for poaching in Yugoslav waters.

Resigned to a hungry morning, the cat rounded the point in the direction of the bathing beach with its colonnade of white huts. The January morning was not yet day. Agaves raised their thorny arms in greeting to the cat; the pines were velvety, the grass soft and pale green against his pads. Snapdragons – but this cat calls them snapdonkeys, being a Dalmatian cat – strewed the ground. Small birds fluttered like butterflies among the bushes. A crow croaked rheumily and the cat, more in frightened play than anything, scared up a sea-eagle — then another; they sailed out over the water, over a coughing fishing-boat, away to the peace of the islands.

Then the cat climbed a hillock to gain a view of the town. Up there was the fort of Spanjola, looking like a burning white jelly-fish; down there the tired houses, shoulder to shoulder. Then the water. The water was wide and still and strewn with islands; first two little ones quite close, then further out larger ones. Furthest of all the horizon was divided up by isles like long grey ships.

The cat stood arching his back in the morning sun on an island among the pine-soft islands of Dalmatia.

Just as he was dropping off to sleep on an empty stomach a pillar of smoke appeared in the north. The boat from Split, thought the cat, now wide-awake. It was just a quarter of an hour from the time the vessel released her smoke on the horizon to the time she put in at the harbour, and though the cat didn't exactly count these minutes, he had a certain route which just filled in the time before the boat's arrival. Down he went to the square where he had loitered an hour before. Opposite Sanmicheli's Gradska Loža the Arsenal peers through its barrel-vault towards the harbour. Beneath this archway there is nearly always a tub or so of herring, but today it was strangely empty. The cat then climbed up towards the theatre, pacing very ceremoniously, knowing it to be a very distinguished theatre — the oldest in the Balkans, indeed, having been built in 1612. He stole through the foyer where the People's Front were holding a morning meeting, and then into the auditorium. Just right for a cat, he thought, but for humans nothing but a puppet-theatre.

Down again to the square. There the Right Reverend the Bishop was conversing with an elderly woman. Better look into the cathedral. This stands at the end of the square and has a pierced Venetian campanile. Everything here is Venice. 'Wonder what sort of a time cats have in Venice,' thought the cat of Hvar. Inside the church — ooh, how dark and cold. Only a few oil lamps were flickering there, hardly able to illuminate themselves.

A bellow came from the entrance to the harbour: the boat from Split. Out of the cathedral dashed the cat, across the square, round the arsenal and away down the avenue of palms. . . .

I was standing on the upper deck, drowsy and queasy in the dawn. The white coasting-steamer slid past some islands. The morning sun set fire to a little town in a bay. On the quay stood a reception-committee of palm-trees. White houses on a mountain-ladder to the sky. I saw a church tower and I saw pines and cypresses. Above the town was a fortress, looking like a quivering white jellyfish perched on a stone.

Passengers were already buffeting their way on board, the sun rose a millimetre, the bell rang for departure.

'Fool!' said the palms to me. 'Here at your feet lies one of the pearls of this earth — and you let it lie. But you'll regret it. The day will come when you clutch your head and say, "I thought I was seeing everything but I saw nothing: I was never in Hvar".'

I don't know how it happened. The next thing I saw was a streak of smoke on the horizon; it was the Dubrovnik boat fading into oblivion. I was in Hvar, breathing the warm, rarefied breath of January.

'You can have our best room,' said the landlord of the Hotel Dalmacija. 'Large bay window, view over the sea. Only 180 dinars — that's cheap. But you've come at quite the wrong time of year, sir; Hvar is a spring town, or a summer one; it's not a place for winter.'

'Will you show me my room?' I asked.

I was the only foreigner in Hvar.

The room was large and light, the bay window broad and sunny. I should be able to sit and write there, bare to the waist in just my shorts. January. Beneath the window ran a road, then rocks, and the transparency of the water. A short pointed bay and, a few hundred yards diagonally across the water, a headland with a church grown fast to its rock. Blossoming almond trees glowed above the monastery walls.

Near me were two islands; on one was a lonely white house. Not a single tree; just stone – white stone – grey, pitiless stone. This was Hvar Prison.

I went out to meet the adventure that is Hvar. I hadn't far to walk. Fifteen hundred people in a Dalmatian town don't need many houses but they do need two or three churches, a cathedral, two strong bastions, each on its own rock, a few renaissance palaces and a harbour-basin to loiter round.

In fact, Hvar was nothing but a harbour framed by houses and a quay. As I went down towards the square by the cathedral I thought of Capri, but Hvar has deeper roots; it belongs to itself, not to a fortune-hunting and eccentric world.

I struggled up a narrow alley; the sun shone down through it from the north-east. Vines rambled and twined over the walls. Apple-trees, lemon-trees. . . . The last slope up to Spanjola was a tropical garden. Two workmen were digging among the plants; one of them laid down his spade, came with me and unlocked the gate of the fort.

Parliamo italiano poco, molto poco, both of us; *percio* we understand each other all the better. Antun Marević was the gardener's name and he told me about the fort. We looked out over the water, pointing out isle after isle; we looked down into the valley, following with a nail-tip the Indian-red road to Starigrad; we shaded our eyes; the three soldiers had reached Napoleone and were dragging the donkey through the gateway.

Antun Marević told his own story. He told of eleven months in an Italian concentration-camp. 'They informed against me because I was a Communist.' He told of his mother and sister who were watched day and night by Italian carabinieri. Of his escape from the camp and through capitulating Italy, of fights with the Partisans, of his wounded leg and more heavy years in Italy, this time in a field hospital.

'I've been given another two years. Then we must take that leg, says the doctor.'

He told of his three children and of his flowers.

'Write home to Sweden,' said Antun Marević, 'and tell them that Yugoslavia is a good country, that Tito is a great man and that Hvar is the most beautiful town in the world.

'Come, I'll show you something,' he said, and he led me into his garden.

He showed me his silk-flowers, his twenty different sorts of cactus, and the date-palms that he was going to plant below Spanjola. And he showed me his toddling three-year-old daughter. He was the happy gardener of Hvar.

With a bunch of antirrhinums and a bag of silk-flower seeds I walked down against the sun through the narrow alley to the harbour.

There I met the prettiest girl in Hvar. She was soft, with broad hips; she was the sea's companion; she smiled and her teeth were like pearls.

'*Gospodin*,' she said. 'You have a camera. No one else in the place has one. Tell me, *gospodin*, would you take a picture of me?'

Who could resist that smile?

She let go her child's hand and the child snivelled off into a garden. They said that its father was a distinguished English lord, which made the lovely girl of Hvar even lovelier and even more respectable.

Now continues the story of the wildcats of Hvar.

The lovely girl sat down on the steps — or the street, whichever you choose to call it. But she couldn't just sit there, posed and stiff; she must hold something in her arms. Why not a cat? Could anyone get hold of a cat?

Fifty honest citizens shook their heads.

Didn't they understand me? I must explain more clearly. I mewed loudly – miaow, miaow – arched my back and hit out with my paws. Fifty grave heads were shaken.

I insisted: the girl *must* have a cat.

'A cat! *Nije, nije;* A goat, a dog, a peacock — but a cat? *Nije, nije!*'

I was obdurate: 'There are cats all over the place — are you all blind? You've only got to pick one up.'

'*Nije, nije!*'

'Very well,' I said. 'Have it your own way. No cat, no photograph. I'll put away the camera.'

That did it. The chance of a free show like this couldn't be allowed to slip by without a struggle.

For half an hour cats were chased through Hvar. This was the day of the great cat-hunt which has become part of the history of Hvar, like the day when the island fell before the troops of Napoleon. But the cats hissed and scratched and bit and the citizens of Hvar returned empty-handed and bleeding. We gave up the attempt.

'See what you've done, *gospodin:*' said an elderly man. 'You should have listened to us. We know the Hvar cats; there are no more vicious cats in all Dalmatia — in all the world, *gospodin.*'

'But we've done what we could,' said another. 'Not a cat, it's true, but it is an animal, and a very quiet one.'

A girl perhaps ten years old, with spectacles and plaits, led forward a goat. A murmur of appreciation ran through the gathering. The whole of Hvar must have been on its feet now. The loveliest girl in Hvar embraced the goat and I took the first picture. One of the cat-hunting bystanders applauded, another joined in, and soon all were clapping.

It was a sensation. Clouds had sailed up over us, but they were soft clouds, cotton-wool clouds, yellow-filter clouds. A boy fetched his rabbit.

'No, no,' I said.

But the citizens of Hvar insisted. So I photographed a rabbit. An elderly man on crutches arrived with a hen.

'No!' I said, as firmly as I could. 'No more animals today.'

But the citizens of Hvar would not yield. I took photographs. Everyone clapped. By now the avalanche had started: an inventory was taken of all the domestic animals in Hvar, and every picture was applauded. A mule, an old woman with a cage of canaries. A donkey with its leg in a splint. A blind dog. A cock, and finally a grass-snake. Every exposure was clapped. I photographed everything — except a cat.

It was Saturday in Hvar — a gala day. The sun shone and clouds scudded before the wind towards the little isle with its prison, the grey-ship islands and the jagged islands on the horizon.

That is the story of the wildcats of Hvar which would not be photographed.

A light breeze blew up from the north-west. The bells of St Francis which I could see from my balcony began ringing with a brittle, glassy sound. Sound-waves and sea-waves met on the rippled surface of the water. A Franciscan friar, white-haired, with a waddling gait and pouting lower lip, showed me into the refectory.

'This is a very remarkable painting,' he said, pointing to a fresco of the Last Supper. 'It was done by the great sixteenth-century painter Matteo Rosselli; no doubt you've heard of him. He was dying when he came to Hvar, but he was cured of his disease here, in this monastery, and painted this by way of thanksgiving. But there are even more remarkable things here. Look at our collection of coins; here you see coins from Greece and Rome, here is some Venetian silver money, here are napoleons — yes, there are coins from every period of Hvar's history, and every one of them was picked up on the island. But there are even more remarkable things in our house. Look at our copies of the Scriptures; see how meticulous, how minute and how precise they are. They were all done by the brothers. But there are even more remarkable things here. Come into the garden. Look at all these medicinal herbs in flower, and smell the almond-blossom! But even more remarkable — look at that cypress; it's very remarkable — the most remarkable thing we have. It has two peculiarities: for one thing it's horizontal. But what is even more remarkable is that it's four hundred years old! Why, do you know, before the war an English film company came here just to photograph our cypress.'

The friar stroked the gnarled branches and one couldn't tell tree from fingers. Against the monastery wall hung the raw egg-yolks of lemon-trees.

'But there are even more remarkable things about this place. Feel the wind — how warm it is. In January. It's already spring with us. There has never been any winter. Isn't it amazing?'

And when evening came that day in Hvar, moonlight poured over the cathedral, the arsenal and the Loggia and over the noblest of the Venetian palaces, Palazzo Hektorovića – decayed now, with washing hanging in its windows – to be caught at last in the Franciscans' remarkable cypress, where it stayed motionless but quivering.

Waves beat below my balcony. Song rose from the water and I stepped out. Fishermen were singing, and their voices followed one another as the swell followed the sea-bed, as gulls followed the swell, as the black sky with its pin-point stars followed the gulls.

What were all the concert-halls in the world beside this vast hall of islands, Adriatic Sea and sooty sky? If art is nature ennobled, what else were these men's songs? You waltzes of Roslag, you accordion-tunes of Bohuslän, what rough throats those are for which you arose from your rocks and Baltic pines! Moon, be silent; accordion, douse your light. Listen to the fishermen from Split!

Each voice was something complete, a perfection: the growling bass, the nectar-filled baritone, the honeyed tenor and the voice with the shrill blare of a trumpet. But no voice predominated; one sound caught hold of the next and blended into a close-woven whole. The singing was like light, and the notes of light can only regain their freedom in the spectrum. Full as the moon, the singing illumined the waves.

And this from lips black with chewing-tobacco. Coarse hands smelling of fishscales. . . .

The brilliance upon the sea fell silent.

'Would I go down and drink a bottle of wine?'

We drank red wine under the moon and solved the riddles of the sea, which are those of life. The boat rocked as lightly as a cradle, caressing the quay. Toni Carić and Matošić Nikse raised their glasses:

'*Skål* for Sweden!'

'And now,' says Matošić, 'we will drink to Tito and Communism,' and I have to drink to Tito and Communism. What of it? Sweden is far away.

The three soldiers who had led their pack-ass up between the cactuses to Napoleone now had leave of absence; they sat on a bollard listening to the singing. The gardener from Spanjola limped up to the boat, and his opulent wife held two babies in her arms. Like a shadow with lithe hips came the lovely girl of Hvar. A cloak rustled; it was the friar from the Franciscan monastery, enticed by the singing. One of the close-cropped little soldiers asked the lovely girl of Hvar for a dance, and the honey-tenor made the faintest hint of a glissando. The Italian seamen on board *La Vittoria* gazed hungrily at us through the darkness. The heels of the guard tapped monotonously.

The few street-lamps faded, and the lights in the tavern beyond the troop of palms went out. The Hvar power-station had finished its five-hour shift. 'We have a very fine generator,' said the waiter of the Hotel Dalmacija. 'It's oil-driven. Unfortunately oil is expensive.'

Only the moon and the singing of the fishermen were left to illuminate nocturnal Hvar.

Then a miracle came to pass. Two green lights sped towards us along the edge of the quay, sprang up like parallel rockets — and I felt something soft in my arms. I stroked fur and heard purring: melodious, serene. . . .

I listened. The fur and the ember-eyes spoke: 'I was lying on my wall and saw the harbour was full of ink. I saw the loom of a boat in the harbour and heard singing. So I tried to sing, and something bubbled up in me. I purred, I couldn't endure this happiness alone — I felt it wasn't only for me. So I padded down to the harbour to purr for somebody else.'

94

Thus spoke the cat from the Spanjola slopes.

And this is the happy ending to the story of the cats of Hvar.

9. DUBROVNIK

FROM the deserted terrace you saw Fort St Ivan: a white flat-iron against the blue silk of Dubrovnik harbour. Here, where came the caravels of old, a few dinghies and the sails of fishing-craft yawned at the morning sun as it rose over Serdj. You saw the dome of the cathedral; you heard the bells ring. The tower turned the hands of its green clock.

The Bishop crossed the square, and there was his brother the greengrocer. And the jetty, the jetty with its red lantern – the jetty of grief and kisses – and beyond it the Adriatic, full of moon; and the Lokrum of Archdukes Max and Rudolf, blacker than a cruiser at night.

But beyond Dubrovnik lurks Gruž, the port. The town of rust-strippers and dying ships. Rustling flags, hulks with gonorrhoea. In this darkness, red stars on the funnels of Yugoslav vessels.

It was here I came at twilight from Hvar of the cats.

It was here I came — here to Dubrovnik; and now that I'm to speak of Dubrovnik my heart fails me. For how can any description of mine be more than a feeble likeness of this pearl of the Adriatic? Even this imperfect image must be commonplace, for any attempt to turn Dubrovnik into literature is doomed to failure. Only the city itself can poise so superbly on the brink of the banal.

Of all my cities Dubrovnik is the most perfect. If I might choose, from among all the places in the world, two in which to live the rest of my life, one would be Paris and the other Dubrovnik. Courage is needed to pursue this train of thought; the mere idea of renouncing these cities brings pain.

Perfection may not be the most important condition for living, but

St Blaise's Day. The relics of the patron saint were carried through the streets. Children kissed the glittering reliquary containing the saint's skull.

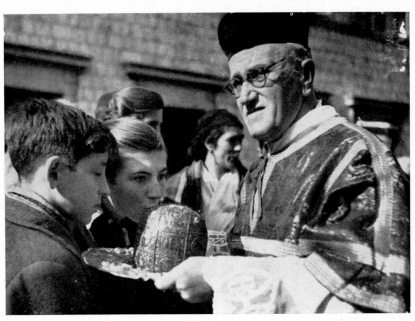

A man from the Konavle valley in national dress.

of Paris and Dubrovnik, Dubrovnik is more nearly perfect. There is
not a stone within its encircling wall that has not been planned, not
a vista uncalculated. No city in the world – no, not even in Italy –
has developed so consistently, yet so freely. There are towns drawn
with ruler and compasses, towns based on the golden rule, on sacred
numbers and proportions, but they are as stiff-legged as dividers.
There are squares and parts of cities governed by the graceful disci-
pline of Dubrovnik, but these architectural highlights of Paris and
Rome – a Place de la Concorde or a St Peter's Square – are at most
episodes in a play of chances.

But Dubrovnik is like a sonnet, whose lines, variously grouped, are
indissolubly bound in a rhythmic whole.

And this is its greatness: to speak no language but that of stone,
and yet be a living organism. The white town, blue-white under the
moon, blue-white under Serdj that is filled with the moon's life;
Dubrovnik, the city without a leaf of living green, yet in itself a
flower. Dubrovnik, the city without neon flourishes, without posters
or shop-signs. Dubrovnik, the city of white stone.

I came here one evening aboard the *Kotor*, docking at Gruž, the
port of dying ships.

On the quay, taxis glared with big eyes at the gang-plank. Together they formed a museum of mobile monuments to the era of the
Dubrovnik millionaires. There were speaking-tubes for the back seats,
but the driver sat in the open, to mark his servile condition. Rusty
marvels.

Then a stately Packard, conveying the Senior Communist Official,
would glide past; for here, where poverty is most evenly distributed,
we find a proletariat and an upper class assessed in horse-power: taxi-
drivers and successful Party men.

Ten dinars for the tram-fare to Pile and the square between the
Kavana Dubravka and the Hotel Posta. This was the first evening in
February.

The city gate opened; over the ditch we went and through the
wall. Little did I think, standing for the first time in the Placa or the

Strado, that I was to stay here for two months. For me Dubrovnik became a prison, but who ever had a lovelier prison than mine?

On that day in February I stood in the Placa at the hour when night pours in over evening. The Placa is broad and several hundred yards long, without pavements. Dubrovnik is a city without pavements, cars or bicycles. There where the Placa ends a tower appears, and in it a green, shining clock-face. The houses along the Placa run in one long façade; the first and second are like the third. A wave of people surged over the Placa to break just in front of me. These people are Dubrovnik; in the violet hours they change into shadows, glide up and down and vanish at last in a darkness of blue-black Indian ink. The lamps are lit – their yellow-white light turns the sky to purple, almost to black – and everyone recognizes everyone else; everyone nods or raises his hat, saying *dobar dan* or *adio*, which in Dubrovnik means good day: just as the girls here and nowhere else in the world say *ajme!* for alas. Every little town in the south has a strolling-place, but none like the one in Dubrovnik.

Here I stood by a domed, sixteen-sided building which looked in the darkness like a miniature observatory and which later, guidebook in hand, I discovered to be Onofrio de la Cava's fifteenth century fountain. Here I beheld that world rolling towards me and breaking at my feet. Here Dubrovnik's great problems are solved: the question of the water-supply, of the library-grant and of the motor-boat service to Lokrum. In the Placa the riddles of the universe are solved and the little problems of the world: the Indonesian crisis is dealt with and France gets a new government. In the Placa intrigues are woven and daughters married off; in the Placa people discuss the week's film showing at the cinema behind the Ploče Gate.

The Placa is everything: the town's newspaper and marriage-bureau, lover's lane, the arena of municipal government, the grapevine — above all, it is a safety-valve against explosions and catastrophes. All conflicts suppressed during the day are released in the Placa; they blow out through this valve. It ensures the even flow of life, without storms or violent outbreaks of passion. It is Dubrovnik's middle way.

I did not yet know the individual shadows in this stream: the mayor, and Ivo Soljka the editor of the local newspaper, once Catholic, then Orthodox and now a Communist star in decline; I still did not know the collector of icons who wrote the reactionary art-notices. Or Zdenko Šapro, the clarinettist at the Gradska Kavana, who trilled the Kivik Polka on an evening in March; or Vesna Barbić, the young woman-director of the Museum of Art, who piloted Göran Schildt to Ombla; or Captain Ivo Dijmović who was hoping that his run-away wife would return from Rijeka. They were all strolling up and down between the Pile gate and the gate to Ploče. A shadow in a beret detached itself from the rest and came up to me.

'My name is Joca Boar, and I'm the town photographer.'

We walked down the Placa.

'You know of course that the Placa was once straits?'

'No; how should I?'

'At that time Dubrovnik was an uninhabited island; the original population lived some miles to the southward, in Greek Epidaurus.'

'Thank you; but you know, I'm rather tired.'

'Tired? Then I must offer you a glass of wine. Wine from Epidaurus. Today it's called Cavtat; it was there that our great painter Bukovac lived.'

An obstinate man, Joca Boar; but the Cavtat wine was sweet and good and the café-owner ever ready with fresh glasses.

'We call this place the Café Imbecili. At one time all the dotty old maids of the town came here and gossiped about the people passing by below. Well, as I said, the town was called Epidaurus, and Dubrovnik was a bird-colony. Then came the migrations and in the seventh century Epidaurus was destroyed. The survivors fled to the rock below Serdj and founded a new city called Ragusa. But on the other side of the sound the Slavs settled, and their town was named Dubrovnik after the Slav word for acorn: *dubrava*. In the twelfth century the straits were filled in, and the result was the Placa and one single city. But the gentry continued to live west of the Placa, and the eastern side became a ghetto. In the evenings those streets were barred off from the Placa, and woe to the Jew who ventured out.'

'Thank you; but I think I'm still a bit tired.'

'Tired?' said Joca Boar. 'Tired, when you come to Dubrovnik? But if you call at my studio tomorrow I'll show you the town.'

I fell asleep that night in the Hotel Dubrovka blissfully unaware that I was to be Dubrovnik's prisoner for two months.

I woke next morning in the same happy ignorance, and went to the *Odjel Unustrašnijih Poslova,* where the Police Superintendent was sitting smoking a cigar and tapping the table with a pencil in boredom when I came in and asked for my passport.

'Your passport?'

'Yes, my passport. The police in Split sent it to the Ministry of the Interior in Zagreb.'

'To the Ministry of the Interior—'

'Yes. My visa had expired and had to be renewed.'

The Superintendent threw out his hands and pronounced with relish the few foreign words he knew:

'*No . . . No . . . Che fare . . . Aspettare. . . .*'

But come again tomorrow.

I must wait until tomorrow. Police Headquarters lay outside the Pile gate, and the road led up to the park. The park was at the top of a cliff; in the swooning depths below — green water. Opposite was Lovrijenac, a white fortress (in the summer they play *Hamlet* in its courtyard). Behind Lovrijenac lay the town, beyond the town Lokrum, where Richard Coeur de Lion sought refuge; beyond Lokrum a green swirl of coastline away towards Cavtat. Beyond that again a white jag into the sky: Orjen. Beyond Orjen, Montenegro.

I took a road down towards the sea. A black padre with a black beard was taking his morning stroll in his black petticoats. A woman guarded her white cow on the hillside. A boy lay on his stomach in a hollow, shooting at three birds with a catapult. For a thousandth of a second they quivered in the air, then vanished.

I came to a convent with a churchyard by the sea.

Oh, but Joca Boar was waiting for me! I went back and met him at the Pile gate.

'What happened to you? And what do you think of Dubrovnik?'

'I've been with the police most of the time, and I fetched my letters from the post office.'

We went down the Placa. The sun stood at eleven o'clock, and although it was February we carried our coats over our arms. On our right was Onofrio's fountain and on our left the Franciscan church and the grave of the poet Ivan Gundulić, author of *Osman*.

'There's a marvellous garden in there, and an apothecary-shop dating from 1318,' Joca Boar told me. 'The third oldest in Europe. Let's go in.'

'Not just now,' I said.

'Are you in a hurry?'

'Not really. In fact, I've never had so much time in all my life.'

We went down to the other end of the Placa, and that river was now bare stone in the sunshine. In front of the gate leading to Ploče, the residential district of the vanished Dubrovnik millionaires, stands Orlando Furioso in stone, a flagstaff at his back.

'That's the Roland of the legend,' explained Boar. 'And the church opposite the church of St Blaise is called the Sponza.'

'I know,' I said. 'The Sponza began by being a warehouse and is now the Public Records Office; between times it was used as a mint and as the seat of the learned academy of Dubrovnik. The name of the architect is Paskoje Milicević and he built it in 1516 and '17. Anything more you'd like to know?'

Boar laughed.

'Where did you learn all that?'

'It's very simple. I read it in a periodical called *Jugoslavija*, which I shall recommend to all who come here. The Sponza is a mixture of Gothic and Renaissance, by the way.'

'If you have time some Sunday afternoon you must look into the courtyard. They dance the *lindjo* there, to the music of the *gusle*. The *lindjo* is a folk-dance from the Konavle Valley which runs southward from Dubrovnik towards Herzegnovi, and the *gusle* is a national instrument with one string. Behind you is the church of St Blaise, who, as you no doubt know, is the patron saint of Dubrovnik.'

'And don't you dare tell me how he became it; I've heard the story three times and read it in two different places.'

'That's not true!'

'Well, no, perhaps not; but it might easily be.'

'Now, a thousand years ago,' began Boar relentlessly, 'the bishop dreamed that the Turks were attacking the city, so he got up and woke the priests and the priests woke the monks and the monks woke—'

'—the people.'

'No, not the people. The monks woke the bellringers and the ringers tolled the bells—'

'—and the people woke up.'

'Exactly. The people closed the gates, one after the other. First the Ploče gate—'

'—and then the Pile gate. So it's St Blaise who stands over all the gates, and SB-Libertas on the flags means St Blaise's Freedom. Isn't that so?'

'You're impossible.'

'Not at all. Not in any way.'

We turned off to the right between the Gradska Kavana and the church of St Blaise and came to the renowned Rectors' Palace. Michelozzo Michelozzi himself, who played so great a part in the rise of the Renaissance in Florence, had a finger in the pie when the Rectors' Palace was built.

The palace, like the Sponza, is something halfway between Gothic and Renaissance, but the mixture of styles is less obvious than in the façade of the Sponza. It has a loggia of seven pillars, of which each capital is different. One is strewn with stone flowers; on another, *putti* dance with garlands in their hands. The third represents an apothecary's shop, where a sick peasant asks for help. The fourth and fifth . . .

'You can see from these pillars,' said Joca Boar, 'that seven architects worked on this palace. Each architect was allowed to carve his own capital, and each capital has its own story. The first—'

'Thank you,' I said, 'It's very kind of you, but I shall learn the stories for myself in time.'

Now the clock in the city tower struck half past one and the sun above Serdj shone slantingly across the façade of the Rectors' Palace. Light flooded the Sponza, as in holy pictures for children. Light soused the church of St Blaise, and in the wet February shimmer the building looked like a toy in graceful, witty baroque. This square between the Placa and the Gradska Kavana, with the Sponza at one end of it and the cathedral at the other – a square not yet mentioned, where someone was practising the organ – was turned into pure lyric in the light from Serdj.

And now the cathedral clock struck half past one; to mark its ponderous dignity it always struck a little later than the rest. The bishop crossed the square with his brother the greengrocer, and shadows played among the capitals of the columns: the angels danced above theirs; the flowers gave forth their scent, if stone flowers may; the friar in his apothecary felt his stiffened limbs relax and he tried to climb the ladder for the bowl of mint-flowers.

But the light could not reach the back wall of the arcade, and in a corner of shivering darkness stood a naked girl embracing a dog.

'That's a grisly-looking statue,' I said.

'You probably don't want to hear the story of it,' said Joca, 'but I shall tell it anyway. That girl was the daughter of a rector, and in old Dubrovnik a rector was the same as a mayor. The rectors were elected for only a month at a time, and this girl was the daughter of one of them. She was betrothed, but unfortunately she had a morbid love of dogs and she forsook her fiancé for a dog. So there she stands as a terrible example. . . . But come into the courtyard. You see that

bust on a pedestal? That's Miho Pracat who lived in the time of
Ferdinand and lent his ships to Isabella's armada. In return he might
ask for anything he liked. But he was tremendously rich already, and
begged for nothing but Isabella's garter. Afterwards he gave all his
money to Dubrovnik.'

The upper floor of the Rectors' Palace ended in a balcony round
the courtyard. It was reached by a broad flight of steps, and above
the door of the great Council Chamber there was an inscription in
stone:

OBLITI PRIVATORUM PUBLICA CURATE

Forget your private affairs and seek the general good.

'Very sound, very fine,' I said. 'All the same, I'm still anxious
about my passport.'

'Why, what's happened to it?'

'Lost in Zagreb,' I answered, and told the story.

'My friend,' said Joca, 'I'm delighted to hear it. It means you'll be
staying here another couple of months. If I know anything about the
ministries in Zagreb, they've put your passport under their pillows.
But surely you're in no hurry? You're young – life is beautiful –
tomorrow is another day, and so is the day after tomorrow. Take it
calmly and wait tranquilly for spring. We do. We wait, you see.
We're all waiting. Dubrovnik in February is a dead town. But stay
till the summer, for then there'll be lovely women here, and music
on the terraces. . . . '

We went back to the Placa.

'You'll be thinking me very boorish,' I remarked, as we leaned on
the bar-counter with our glasses of *rakija*. This is bitter brandy dis-
tilled from what's left after the grapes have been pressed. 'You've
been trying, out of pure kindness, to show me Dubrovnik. You
wanted to take me up on to the ramparts and drag me into each and
every one of your forty-one churches. And instead of thanking you
I've been almost rude. I owe you an explanation.

'All you've said to me and all you've wanted to tell me is very interesting. But none of it's new; I can find it all set out more accurately and concisely in *Jugoslavija* or in the German booklet I bought this morning at Putnik's for seventy-five dinars. Isn't it a pity you should waste your time on me — or waste it in explaining what has already been said?'

'Two more *rakijas*,' said Joca Boar. He made no comment, and I went on:

'Every traveller has to collect his own material, whether historical or artistic. He has to sort out what interests *him*, and scrap the rest. All you've told me and would like to tell me really does interest me, but I might have been listening to you out of mere politeness. I can't expect everyone to feel as I do. If I write a book about Yugoslavia, it doesn't mean I want to write an exhaustive history of Dubrovnik. That alone would fill a book. Above all, I don't want my readers at home, who have no immediate experience of these squares and streets and fountains and churches, to yawn and skip two or three pages at a time. Obviously I can't ignore the material – the cultural and historical background – but with every town, shore and sea I must discard what I think is unessential, and shape my book with the little bit that's left. I shan't be writing a novel – worse luck – and I'm tied down by historical fact and my five senses, but I mustn't shirk the subjective approach on that account. My presentation of the journey may turn out to be one-sided, but I must, in my capacity of Me and Myself, throw highlights on certain aspects and leave the rest in darkness or dusk. In each case I must choose a standpoint. If it's to be a book about Yugoslavia it won't be a hand-book; it'll be more of a ground-book: an attempt at synthesis, a summary of what I believe and believed to be important. Anyone who travels must choose his point of view, but it doesn't amuse me to provide dull, neutral material for other travellers to turn into personal experience. . . . Now you know where you are with me, and now let's contradict it all and climb the ramparts to count churches and fortifications.'

By a stair at the Ploče gate we climbed up on to the wall. There was a broad footway, and to the south lay a stretch of Adriatic coast which by now had become part of my consciousness. White cliffs dropped sheer into burning blue water, and above them were stone-pines, pale green, almost sun-yellow grass and the green and silver hoods of olive-trees. Along the rock wall, the flames of cypresses. A blue bus, its paint peeling, hummed along the twisting road in a cloud of fine dust. Sheep grazed on the slopes; cactuses and agaves stood on guard at the roadside. These agaves, with arms like soft, fleshy saw-blades – some in bloom with their flowers on long sticks – gazed down undizzied into the depths. But agaves bloom only once, and many of them were already weighed down by the knowledge that they must now dry up and perish in the sun.

Nearer Dubrovnik: Ploče, with its millionaires' villas – now con-fiscated – embedded in gardens. There cherry-trees aired their pink skirts. There stood the Hotel Argentina and beside it the Villa Scheherazade with its glittering blue cupola, its Moorish windows, Persian rugs, lakes and swimming pool and its boat-house blasted out of the rock: a Baltic millionaire's dream of Arcadia and the Orient.

This is where Eden stays, and Eleanor Roosevelt, when they visit Dubrovnik. But from the ramparts the town itself is a white town no longer, but a city of pale pink tiles. To look out over Dubrovnik is to look at a sea caught between tumult and mirrored calm.

'Since you're going to be with us some time longer, you must come to the St Blaise festival,' said Joca Boar before we parted. 'Every year on the 2nd of February we celebrate the bishop's dream and the miraculous preservation of Dubrovnik. But as you know, the Catholic Church and the Communists have different ideas about some things. The 2nd February used to be Dubrovnik's great feast and holiday, with processions through the streets; but the Communists turned St Blaise's Day into an ordinary working-day, so the bishop retorted by moving the feast to the first Sunday after the 2nd. You simply must see it. But of course it's not what it was.'

Next morning at nine o'clock I went again to the house behind the palm-trees and Radio Stanice, in Pile — that building where the policeman lounged against the wall and a sign by the door said: *Odjel Unuštranijih Poslova.*

'Any news of my passport?'

'Your passport?'

'Yes, my passport.'

'We know nothing of any passport.'

'Don't you recognize me?'

'We've never seen you before.'

Was this fellow quite right in the head? Could he really be chief of the Dubrovnik police? And his secretary — she spoke Italian and I had talked to her the day before. Or was I dreaming?

'But I was here yesterday.'

'Oh, are you the one who came yesterday? About the passport in Zagreb?'

'That's it.'

'Why couldn't you say so before? One moment.'

The girl went out of the room, to return in a minute or two.

'No, there's no passport here. You'd better come again tomorrow.'

'Am I expected to stay here for the rest of my life?'

The superintendent threw out his arms:

'Che fare . . . Aspettare. . . . '

What could I do but wait? I went back next day: Have you heard anything? Nothing. Next day: Nothing yet. Next day – Saturday – Come again on Monday. I went back on Monday morning: Well? Not a word from Zagreb. What am I to do? Why, wait of course — what do you expect *us* to do? Wire Zagreb. We've wired Split and they know nothing about it there.

A week passed, and part of the next.

The police chief deplored and consoled:

'Che fare . . . Aspettare. . . . '

I settled down in Dubrovnik as if I were to stay here for a lifetime.

I woke in the mornings when the women from the Konavle Valley sold cloths, apples, bread, mats and wine to the women of Dubrovnik.

Below my south window lay the vegetable market. I could see the dome of the cathedral and look right down the street to the Rectors' Palace and three of its seven columns.

Twice a day I ate at Pero Lujak's in the second side-street beyond the Sponza leading down to the Placa. Just after twelve noon the sun would hang for a minute at the end of the street; and then balconies glittered and windows sparkled. The steps up to the ramparts shone like piano-keys. Then the little street darkened again in a greasy darkness.

Mamma Lujak cooked. Papa Lujak talked politics and fishing. Ante the waiter was called the Chinaman. Mamma Lujak inspected the fish, Papa Lujak shifted a plate here and there. The Chinaman who had once been a corporal waited upon us with right turn and left turn. Mamma Lujak was big and fat, Papa Lujak small, round-shouldered, unshaven, with cropped grey hair. The Chinaman's pot-belly wobbled. Papa Lujak had more dirt under his nails than anyone else in Dubrovnik. The rag-tag and bobtail of the town hung round the bar and Papa Lujak gave them the scrapings of the saucepans. Papa Lujak's son was at the Embassy in Rome, and Papa Lujak was whispered to be the wealthiest man in all Dubrovnik.

The soaks of Dubrovnik stood at the bar, hawking and spitting, but Lujak's fish was famed throughout Yugoslavia. And I pay homage to Pero Lujak of Dubrovnik for the sake of the *calamare*, the cuttlefish; of the langoustes and crabs, the little fried sardines; the Sanpiero, or plaice; and the lettuce — the clear, pale green lettuce.

At Pero Lujak's I met my best friends: Captain Ivo Dujmović and Pero Šutić the engineer. But I name them with hesitation. They both asked me not to involve them in any book of mine; yet on the other hand we were openly in each other's company for two months, so it seems needless to suppress their identity.

Arthur Koestler in his autobiography writes of his 'gurus': the two men who led him to Communism. One was a Yugoslav who between the wars went under various assumed names. To protect him, Koestler gives him yet another alias, but describes him so minutely as to make it obvious that he is none other than the editor of *Jugoslavija*, Otto Bihajer-Merin. Otto Bihajer-Merin is a slippery, soft character, and when I read that chapter aloud to the Authors' Society in Belgrade – Koestler is banned in Yugoslavia! – no one could imagine how he could have fooled so intelligent a writer as Koestler for three or four years. Those who listened were delighted by the malicious portrait, and it could have done Merin no harm to be called by his proper name.

Neither Ivo Dujmović nor Pero Šutić was a Communist. How many in Yugoslavia were? How many were there in Dubrovnik, that most reactionary of all towns? But Ivo Dujmović and Pero Šutić were not interested in politics. Dujmović lived on his pension and Šutić worked in an office. There was a tacit understanding between us to avoid dangerous topics as one would avoid a clump of stinging-nettles. Dujmović played bridge twice a week and Šutić collected uncancelled French postage-stamps. What else we talked of I can't remember exactly; no doubt the weather, natural disasters, foreign visitors to the town, the butter-seller who was sentenced to two years' imprisonment for tampering with a seven-year-old girl, weddings and funerals — and this alone would have filled a book. We used to meet in the Placa at twilight and have dinner together, and then coffee at the Imbecili, or the Dubravka, outside the Pile gate. The rest of the evening we would spend at the Gradska Kavana.

As I mentioned earlier, the Gradska Kavana stands just by the Ploče gate. It consists of two halves: one overlooks the church of St Blaise and the Orlando statue, and here there were always some old men in black winter overcoats playing chess, the prostitute who was called Lili Marlene, and her peroxided sister, who had just returned from an unsuccessful winter season in Zagreb. The whores of Yugoslavia are to be found in the kavanas of the big hotels, and they're for ever on the move, from hotel to hotel, from town to town. A few steps down from the upper half of the Gradska Kavana there is a large room with pillars, ending in three arches full of windows. These arches look on to a terrace, and below the terrace lies Dubrovnik's retired harbour with its drowsy green sails, and in the background

Fort St Ivan in which is housed the Maritime and Folk-Culture Museum. Behind St Ivan the jetty; the jetty of heartbreak and kisses, *la porporela*; the jetty with the red lantern. The lower half of the Gradska was once Dubrovnik's ship-building yard, and here one night in March the clarinettist Zdenko Šapro played the Kivik Polka. On Saturday evenings there were dances. Here we would come, then, Ivo Dujmović, Pero Šutić and I, and when *il capitano* had drunk half a litre of white wine from Šipan, an island north-west of Dubrovnik, he would grow lyrical and talk of the great oceans and the coasts he would never see again.

One evening *il capitano* took me back to his house and showed me his great vases from the East Indies, and his ivory elephants, and at Easter Pero Šutić invited us to a special dinner. They lived in their villas in Ploče, but these Ploče villas mourn their past, their soft rugs and the patrician seclusion of their arbours. The villas of Ploče are ghettos. The villas of Ploče have been taken over by gardeners and mechanics and God knows what, says the old lady with the mauve hair who was once governess in the household of Alexander, but who now wanders homeless among the roses.

Largest of all was Banac's villa. I believe he spelt his name like that, but I'm not sure. Banac was a fantastic man with a fantastic amount of money. He had a summer villa at Cavtat, and built a road to it; he also intended to build a bridge over to Lokrum, but luckily the war intervened. His villa is concealed by a high wall on the way to the Konavle Valley. Behind the wall is a sunken garden designed for a central fountain. A glass door opens into an entrance hall, from which a staircase leads directly to the great banqueting hall, where the windows rise from the marble floor to the ceiling. A palace of great rooms, courtyards and terraces. It was from one of these deserted, sun-white terraces that I surveyed all Dubrovnik, the harbour of the caravels and the cathedral dome.

But where is Banac?

Banac is dead. One day soon after the war the Partisans came and threw out all his precious porcelain and linen, while half Dubrovnik stood around and filled its string bags. Later it appeared that the porcelain was worth millions, and today it is sought for all over the town, and taken back; for Banac's villa has been nationalized and turned into an art-gallery. This is the gallery of which Vesna Barbić is director, and on her terrace I rounded off my imprisonment, with all the blue Adriatic before me, while warm winds ruffled the pages of Dundo Maroje, Marin Drzić's great folk-comedy. Dundo Maroje is the play about poor Uncle Maroje of Dubrovnik, who sends his nephew to study in Rome, and then hears tales from there of the wildest dissipation. Yugoslavs say of Marin Drzić that he was a Shakespeare before Shakespeare and a Molière before Molière.

The Police Superintendent was still full of sympathy: it was not his fault, he would have liked to help me, but snow had blocked the line between Zagreb and Split — so what could he do? He was no weather-god. The roads from there to Dubrovnik were impassable and the airfield was under water; also the telegraph wasn't working. No passport.

'*Che fare . . . Aspettare. . . .* '

Then came St Blaise's Day.

The night before, the sky had been slashed to ribbons by lightning and hail rattled on the roofs. In the morning the Placa was as shiny as ice on a thawing river. The Chevalier Roland raised his bare flag-staff. But on the stroke of eleven the procession moved out of the cathedral.

First came the men from the village of Čilipi, their red costumes glittering with silver thread and silver buttons; then five priests monotonously chanting: '*Ave . . . Ave . . .* ' Next the archbishop, bearing a reliquary of gold and precious stones; in the reliquary was the head of St Blaise. Now followed priests and monks from the Dominican and Franciscan monasteries. All the fifteen thousand inhabitants of Dubrovnik flocked along the route of the procession, which moved majestically up the Ulica od Puca, round Onofrio's fountain by the Pile gate and then into the Placa.

The relics were besieged with kisses. Old men and women hobbled up to the bishop and touched the reliquary with their lips. Children were led forward by their mothers, dim-sighted and crippled mothers were led forward by their children. With a holy though monkeylike smile Bishop Butorac wiped the saint's head with a white handkerchief.

But in one of the windows stood Šoljka, head of the Dubrovnik radio station and editor of the Dubrovnik weekly paper. Šoljka was pale today, but those who kissed the reliquary were seized with fright when they saw his eyes watching from the window.

When the procession reached the Sponza it turned off to the right, causing the crowd to divide, and glided up the steps of St Blaise's church. Inside, candles were burning and floodlights illuminated the silver miniature over the altar: St Blaise with Dubrovnik in his arms. And just as the cortège stepped out through the door facing the Rectors' Palace, the miracle that all had been hoping for occurred. Not a great miracle, perhaps, but certainly a sign. Bishop Butorac made a hasty sign of the cross, and seeing this the priests did the same, then the monks.

For like a curtain the clouds had parted. Whence came the wind? The sun flung a lance at Dubrovnik. The last steps past the Rectors' Palace were bathed in sunshine, and gold and ruby fires made a nimbus round the reliquary. But at the very instant when the tabernacle containing the great casket of relics swayed into the church, the clouds closed their curtains. The sky flashed a violet signal and thunder darted a tongue of lightning over the hills. With the crash came rain, heavy and relentless.

After St Blaise's Day followed the days of waiting. The passport was as remote as ever, and without it I could not get permission to leave Dubrovnik. From Gradac, the municipal park, I saw Orjen and beyond Orjen lay Montenegro. I longed to go there, but for me Montenegro was a forbidden land. Days of waiting: walks up to the fort on the summit of Serdj, and the village of Bosanka at its back; expeditions too into the surrounding country, and it's these I want to

Montenegrin donkey. (*Below*) Ombla, a part of Arcady.

An old Montenegrin. He hoisted the flag of Montenegro at Scutari.

tell of: of my trips to Čilipi in the Konavle Valley, to Cavtat and to Ombla.

Niko Kuzmić, the young agronomist of Dubrovnik, roamed from village to village with a briefcase under one arm and an umbrella under the other, wearing shoes that were far too big for him and stuffed with paper. He was a little Chaplin, full of illusions about mankind's capacity for betterment, waging war on phylloxera. Together we arrived at Čilipi. By the church, opposite the tavern and the post office a mule was waiting; it lacked the energy even to switch away the flies. Čilipi had always been the wealthiest place in the Konavle Valley; before the war the village owned ten cars and twenty motorcycles. Now, not one.

At Gospoda Vazilić's we drank *rakija* – two big glasses – and there were dried figs to go with it. Afterwards we put the blame on our weak stomachs and on having already drank too much. Cabbage and pork simmered on the stove.

In the People's House Niko urged the peasants to do battle with the phylloxera, while his audience lounged over the tables, picked their noses and chewed fag-ends.

'Phylloxera,' said Niko, thumping the desk, 'phylloxera is eating up your money.'

'Fancy! Is that what happened to it?' signalled my right-hand neighbour.

The church bells were ringing, and blending with Niko's voice came the chant of a funeral procession moving uphill to the church.

'Slippery sort of fellow, the one they're burying,' whispered my left-hand neighbour. 'Used to have too much land. Strong Catholic. Not a Communist.'

The air outside was fresh and cool and already rosy with twilight. There was snow on the mountains. The bells resounded in the windowpanes between the wine-growers and the funeral. First came priests and a big cross, then four men bearing the coffin on their shoulders. Among those following the dead man was Gospoda Vezilić. She had on her best clothes: black skirt, white apron folded over her stomach and a broad sash that made her bust swell majestically; on that bust dangled a yellow tassel. Big gilt rings in her ears and a starched kerchief on her head. But girls and unmarried women wore, in token of their maiden state, a red hood and a cake-tin-lid with embroidered edges; and the girls of Čilipi – the girls of the Konavle Valley in general – are taller, straighter and fairer than the girls anywhere else in Yugoslavia. For it's said that the nobles of Dubrovnik – in the days when Dubrovnik had nobles – sought their mistresses in the Konavle Valley.

The funeral cortège moved into the church and Niko went on speaking; but there's a time for phylloxera, a time for burying and a time for Prince Carnival. For seven years Prince Carnival had been in prison among the reactionaries, but now he was free and he struck up under the rafters with three instruments: double bass, mandoline and flute. It was like the fabulous dressing-up sessions of our childhood, in an attic full of discarded gowns and the secrets of mysterious trunks. Cowboys danced in long underpants and negroes wore blacking on their faces.

Lilac dusk filled the Konavle Valley. Olive groves and cypresses, stone pines and flocks of sheep were veiled in violet as we were lulled homeward in the Dubrovnik bus — I and the apostle of viticulture, Niko Kuzmić. But on another day I went to Cavtat, and Cavtat lies somewhat north of Čilipi, between Čilipi and Dubrovnik.

It was in Cavtat that the dirty icon-collector of Dubrovnik kept his mistress, a sixty-year-old ex-prima ballerina. He visited her every Saturday. It was Cavtat that Joca Boar had spoken of as Epidaurus, the fountainhead of Dubrovnik. It was the inhabitants of Epidaurus that had to flee helter-skelter from the attacking Avars. It was they who built Ragusa on a cliff some miles to the north, and then mingled blood and fire beyond the arm of water, now the Placa.

Cavtat bore the mark of death on its forehead: abandoned Epidaurus slipped long ago into the sea during an earthquake. Beneath clear, still water the sunken city rests in a green glimmer. Fish whisk their silver past fallen columns and the marble eyes of statues. And above the surface, vertigo: the vertigo of sailing over depths of a thousand years or more, over an Atlantis which, though vanished, can yet be sensed and glimpsed in another element.

On the quay I was pursued by a stubbly-bearded man in boots and the dirty cap of a seaman. He looked a shady type.

'I'm the official guide of Cavtat,' he explained, spitting through the gap in his upper teeth. 'Unfortunately I can't take you into the home of our great painter, the late Bukovac, as the daughter has gone into Dubrovnik to do her shopping. But I'm the only one in Cavtat who has the key of the mausoleum, and that's where we're going now.'

A thick tongue of land licked the sea. There, under tall cypresses, lay the graveyard; and there stood the mausoleum, a round building of white stone. The entrance was guarded by two elegant caryatids; this was a gateway to inter-war Yugoslav art, but the gateway itself was from an epoch that still took the human scale for its measure. At a turn of the guide's big key the bronze doors yielded and the chill of death's kingdom came to meet us.

Slender, ethereal marble figures blended indissolubly with the soft white light from above, with the Greek cross and the three chapels beneath the arching dome. Beneath the dome too lay the Rašić family, of Dubrovnik, the last of whose members died within two years of one another. The Rašićs — the shipping-magnates. Spanish influenza carried off the head of the family in 1918, also his son and daughter. In 1919 sorrow took the widow. But before this she had commissioned Meštrović to design the Cavtat mausoleum. Ivan Meštrović was young then. Later he became world-famous, and is a Carl Milles in more than one respect. But his sixty-five-foot-high studio in Zagreb is deserted; he lives in the United States and refuses to come back. Immediately after the war a Communist writer, a friend of Meštrović's, promised to tempt him home and was sent after him, equipped with money and a passport. But he remained over there too, and wrote a malicious book about Tito's Yugoslavia.

In the Rašić mausoleum, the work of Meštrović's youth, with its statue of the Blessed Virgin in untouched beauty and its crucified Christ under a timeless top light, art bids farewell to man. Those drawn-out figures have lost every semblance of humanity; they are insubstantial as ideas. This is the contradiction in Meštrović and his time, and it is a contradiction that turns the world of 'isms' into a necessary refuge.

Cavtat is a dead place. The keeper of the keys stood outside the mausoleum, made water, and did up the last fly-button with a sublime gesture. Cavtat was a dead place full of echoes: the audible echo of the convicts' pick-axes where the new water-main was to be laid, and the inaudible one, the echo of submerged Epidaurus. From the graveyard I could see Dubrovnik as a white belt; and between noon and two o'clock Cavtat's harbour lay clean-swept; there was no one to be seen, only the drifting shadows of huge clouds. Emptiness, the harbour, the marble mausoleum with its inward and outward death; the noise of snoring through a window, the consciousness that somewhere in the sea a Roman city lay sleeping with water in its lungs. The daughter of the famous painter Bukovac had gone into Dubrovnik. Nor did anyone answer when I knocked at the door of the library, which a wealthy Maecenas and bibliophile had presented to Cavtat some time in the last century. In Cavtat the village idiot was a woman and she chased me with flapping arms and toothless cries; but I dodged and she vanished, incapable of turning round or changing her direction.

In such a place, seconds are drops which at long intervals, one by one, fall into a glass that has no bottom.

But on the third and last trip, a square, sky-blue bus stumbled past the quays of Gruž, to which no one returns if he can help it. Then up the river towards Ombla, past the oil-cisterns of Jugonafta where grey soldiers stand guard. The bus bounced alongside the water. The terminus is called Komolac, and at that time I knew nothing and heard no fiddle playing. But a faint, rushing sound reached me; it was the river forcing its way out of the rock, to become gentle, meek or weary after its tussle, and throw its arms round an island. Pity anyone allergic to cypresses here, for even on the island they stand as solemn as tombstones, without a quiver. But here the symbols of death have blunted their points. Swans lay becalmed. There was the church of Prijevor, the village opposite Komolac, and here the sweet-smelling garden of the monastery. Below the church bobbed a rowing-boat. A hundred watercourses that had not wanted to join the river played their own strings as they broke from the mountain. And through this paradise clattered a train with two puffing engines, one at each end, on its way to Sarajevo, dropping a white cloud down the southern rock wall. Yet even this marvel became at last a part of Arcady. For Ombla is cut off from the outside world; it's a corner jutting into an unreality from which there is no outlet, a water-filled furrow in the rock; and in this furrow the retired English naval officer had moored his boat. Growing old had meant for him the chance of coming nearer the sea, nearer the sea-gods and the gods of wine. For this is the necessity: not to sail, but to sail further.

I was not allowed to go beyond Cavtat, Čilipi and Ombla. Days turned to weeks, weeks to a month, then another week, and a week added to that, and still the same negative reply from the house near the Gradac park. Joca Boar said, 'My friend, tomorrow is another day and you're young and life is lovely, especially in Dubrovnik. Why not stay for ever?'

And so I became one of those who walked in the Placa and said *dobar dan* and *adio*.

I measured time by the blossoming fruit-trees. First the January of the almonds; the February of the cherries; then came a March of flowering wild apricot. At dusk, swallows tumbled about the tower of the town hall before heading north. The limestone houses began quivering in the sun. One day the *Oslofjord* put in at Gruž; the Putnik buses went down to the port at dawn and through the gates of the city came four hundred Hawaii shirts over fat bellies, mauve ladies with silver-blue hair, and freckly young women. The parents of the freckly young women sat at home in the States, keeping their fingers crossed for their daughters: the Mediterranean cruise was their last bid in the marriage-market. Never had Dubrovnik been so 'nice,' so 'charming'; for ten days beforehand the place had been in a fever of excitement. The price of Turkish coffee and mass-produced *gusles* was hastily doubled. The Gradska Kavana laid tables for lunch and we, the aborigines, stood at the windows overlooking the verandah and gaped. At street-corners and in squares there was folk-dancing, and the passengers on the *Oslofjord* returned to America convinced that the people of Dubrovnik did nothing but dance the *lindjo* day and night.

Next morning when we woke up, the shop-windows were empty, and the Placa strewn with chewing-gum and empty packets of Chesterfield.

That was the morning that Putnik rang up and asked me to go to the Police Station to fetch my passport, and I went, and there sat the Police-Superintendent with a 'what did I tell you' look in his eye. He handed me my passport and I left the police-station with a visa valid for two months.

And I went on living in Dubrovnik.

10. LUČA MIKROKOSMA

IVO DULČIĆ the painter and I were having a discussion. . . .
There were many painters in Dubrovnik: Štipe Baković who
painted Tito-portraits for the Trades Unions and invited Swiss
girls to drink wine in his studio so as to paint them naked. There
was Politika who lived in Bosanka, the mountain village above
Dubrovnik. It was of his exhibition in the souvenir-shop opposite the
Rectors' Palace that the old icon-collector wrote: 'His work sums up
the best of today's painting.' There was Antun Masle the drawing-
master, who felt he had a vocation, but was one of those who haven't.
In Dubrovnik they called his studies of nudes 'pictorial masturba-
tion'. There was only one painter in Dubrovnik: Ivo Dulčić.

We sat in the Gradska Kavana, by the great window-arches overlooking the terrace. From across the bay could be heard the bells of
Svetji Jakob's monastery. We talked about travelling. At one time
Ivo Dulčić longed to go to Paris; war prevented this, and peace
brought with it currency-difficulties, and much else besides. He had
to stifle that longing. He dug in his mother's vineyard at Boninovo,
north of the town. He painted the slopes running up to Serdj and
Bosanka, he painted Lokrum like a huge fiery whale in the sea. He
was without money but he had to paint; and when he was neither
painting nor digging in the vineyard he sat drinking in the tavern.

'What good does all your roaming do you?' he demanded scornfully. 'Are you any the wiser or better for it? You're chasing an
illusion, my friend.'

'One could tell you were from Dubrovnik,' I said. 'I don't believe
that anyone who belongs here can tear himself away. Why didn't you
stay in Zagreb? You had every chance there; you had made a name
for yourself.'

'A name!' he snorted.

We sat in silence.

What he was thinking I don't know, but I reflected: That's the danger of staying still, anywhere in the world, with any one thought, under any one star. Stones, houses and soil hold one in chains. Dubrovnik had become my Islands of the Blessed. Where was my itch to find new angles on the world? I was exactly where I was when I started, only in another place. Days swallowed days and time grew sluggish and distended. I had ceased seeing and begun to live, as one lives in every town and village; unconsciously, in market-place and café, to the singing of drinking-songs; while clouds – the pursued, the striven-for – gathered themselves into mighty flocks high among the hills, and drifted away, leaving the sheepdogs to bark in vain among the rocks.

The motor-boat for Lapad chugged out of the harbour.

Could Ivo Dulčić read my thoughts?

'I agree with you that one must travel,' he said. 'But why to Paris or Rome? Haven't I light enough here? Haven't I my cactuses and my sea and my harbour with its sails? Think of a hundred and fifty years of Hellas — what a fantastic journey that is! Or think of that wise old fellow Kant.'

He was speaking slowly, pushing the words out three or four at a time, almost incoherently:

'I believe that all . . . the great voyages of discovery . . . have been made . . . in a microcosm where . . . the water of time seemed to stand still . . . and all that has happened to us . . . in an external sense . . . has been . . . unimportant . . . Luča Mikrokosma . . . the Light of Microcosmos. . . . '

'What did you say?'

'Oh — a poem by Petar Njegoš. . . . '

My longing for Montenegro was now renewed. Again I climbed the cliff opposite Lovrijenac. Far away to the southward, beyond Dubrovnik and the blue ridges round the Konavle Valley, white Orjen thrust its spike into the sky. Beyond lay Montenegro.

I said a hasty goodbye to my friends, and equipped with letters of introduction I trundled away in the blue bus one morning to Konavle and towards Herzegnovi, the golden, palm-soughing port of Montenegro. Herzegnovi turns its face to the south, to the entrance of the famous fjord called Boka Kotorska, Kotor's Mouth, which cuts far inland to the town of Kotor at the foot of the main massif of Montenegro. But despite its villas and terraces, despite its year-long mild climate, Herzegnovi cannot in any way be compared with Dubrovnik; it lacks Dubrovnik's enclosed beauty. It is merely a beautiful place; a beautiful place with Greek and Roman traditions. But there are so many lovely places along the coast, and either Greece or Rome has been godmother to all of them. Why choose Herzegnovi for the end or climax of one's journey?

I had to go on; to follow the Boka Kotorska in, towards the secrets of Luča Mikrokosma. But according to the timetable the *Partizan* wouldn't arrive at Herzegnovi for another hour, so I could lunch at leisure and then look at the town for an hour or two. A fat man sat down at my table.

'Welcome to Herzegnovi,' he said. 'May I be allowed to show you the most beautiful view in the world?'

I went with him along the coast road, and where it swings round until it almost overhangs the water I could see right across to the range where the fjord divides.

'Isn't it delightful?' said the fat man.

'Quite enchanting,' I said, to please him.

He had a notebook in his hand and he jotted down everything I said.

'Enchanting, yes — it has grandeur, hasn't it? And where are you bound for next? Where are you from? Why don't you stay in Herzegnovi for the rest of your life?'

Sunlight flooded down and the date-palms shook their ostrich-necks. We returned to the town, through the arch under the campanile and down the steps to the square.

'You must take a photograph of that. Isn't it beautiful?'

'Very beautiful.'

He wrote: 'Very beautiful. A campanile unique in style and character. Quite so.'

A warning signal rolled across the water: the *Partizan* was on her way in. My farewell was brief.

The fat man clutched at my shirt with stubby fingers.

'But sir — are you leaving us already? Won't you stay?' His voice had a ring of hysteria.

But the gangplank had already been drawn in; I had to jump the rail, while the fat fountain-pen remained on the quay waving his notebook and shouting, 'Your name — your address! Do you write? For what paper?'

And my answers flew across to him as the foaming furrow widened between us; they rebounded against the jetty and against all that wooded strip of coast, with its snugly-nestling villas, sweet-smelling flowers, palms, pines and gardens — and the fat man was still writing.

I suspected that I'd committed a mortal sin in not staying in Herzegnovi. For Herzegnovi was not only what it is called in tourist folders, the Pearl of the Boka Kotorska, but the world's most splendid, most precious jewel — at least to the man on the quay. For where is the local patriot who does not regard his birthplace as the fairest place on earth? To the native, beauty is scaled upon the hills and the sea of childhood.

'That was the head of the Herzegnovi tourist-bureau,' said a voice beside me. 'He gets a commission on every tourist that he can produce written proof of having shown round the town.'

I turned, and there at my side with his hands on the rail stood a man who might have been stand-in for Groucho Marx. He wore plus-fours and had a rucksack at his feet. Black, bushy eyebrows overhung the deep-set eyes, and his moustache tickled his black cigar. This was the leading landscape-photographer of Montenegro. He knew every peak of Orjen, every cleft under Lovćen, every stone of

Vrmac. His house was at Prcanj, a few miles from Kotor, beneath the shadow of Vrmac. Now he stood at the rail with tears moistening his moustache.

'Look at my lovely peaks,' he said, and his finger followed the ring of hills.

With annihilating swiftness the *Partizan* washed the shores of Boka Kotorska with her wake. The loveliness of Herzegnovi was already a thing of the past, and we glided into a mightier, sterner, more dynamic world. The mountains reared their ponderous bodies from the water.

It was scenery in the grand manner, almost like a Norwegian fjord.

The surface of the water froze to dark bottle-glass.

'Look at my beautiful cities!' said the leading landscape photographer of Montenegro.

But their beauty was the beauty of death. Their houses were skulls; their fountains had lost their echo under cobwebs. Their citizens had died, appointing decay as their only heir. Like white, gnawed skulls of horses the cities of Boka Kotorska rested against the black mountain: the Risan of the Illyrians; and this, the city of mute bells, Perast, which had once so fine a naval academy that Peter the Great sent thither the sons of the boyars.

Off Perast lie two little islands: Svetji Djordje and Gospa od Srpjela. They are so small that they have only room for a church each, those of St George and of the Virgin. Round them stands a bodyguard of tall, straight cypresses.

'Do you see that little boat pulling across to Svetji Djordje?' said the photographer. 'That's the overseer making his weekly inspection of the churches. Put a frame round boat, water, island and cypresses — now can you see that it was here Böcklin was inspired to paint his Island of Death? At least so tradition says.'

Cool as the waters of Acheron were these waters. And now dusk fell. A sudden dusk, all-desiring, throwing its shadow across the water and filling the hollow with a grey mist which did not, like other twilights, smell of violets. Black eagles rose in the mountains and glided down the hillsides, covering Boka Kotorska with the night of their wings. The eyes of lamps, half-closed, blinked over the still water.

Though it was not more than eight o'clock, Kotor rested in ironbound sleep behind its massive wall. The low, leaning, thickset tower bore up the big clockface like a weary Cyclops. A lorry sighed up the zigzag road over Lovćen to Cetinje. Spiders wove their nets in the heavy darkness.

The *Partizan's* screw ceased beating and we heard only the whispering which is the quiet of mountain night. Then a sliding rustle; with our funnel floodlit we came alongside the quay.

A dream – inconceivable, fantastic – faded.

I nipped a louse in my bed at the Hotel Slavija, and got up. It was already noon and Kotor was bathed in sunshine. Behind the hotel hundreds of donkeys were waiting, and behind the donkeys rose the mountains. This was the radiant climax of the day.

At about three the Dubrovnik bus came in, waited for an hour, and then started on the next leg of its journey to Cetinje, the former capital of Montenegro. The road twisted and writhed like a giant snake up the slopes of Lovćen. Donkeys on their way up to the mountain villages dropped rusty echoes like anchor-chains into the ravines. Deeper and deeper sank Kotor. Vrmac's back, insurmountable from a frog's eye view, became a black roof. The whole of Boka Kotorska opened out, a silver, glinting fish with white and pink scales that were houses. The driver stopped the bus and told me to get out and take photographs.

'Because you know, when Bernard Shaw drove up the Lovćen road he said he'd never seen a more tremendous view in the whole world.'

Higher and higher we climbed, and after a dozen hairpin bends we reached the sky. The air was quite blue. On one side we beheld the whole of Boka Kotorska, looking now like somebody's appendix, while to the west lay the Adriatic. And in the distance, like a glittering pin-head, Herzegnovi.

At three thousand feet the snow met us. Donkeys balanced along the precipices. We drove a few hundred yards, halted to let a few of them pass, and then on for another hundred. We passed an old man with a drooping white moustache; his legs dangled comfortably at his donkey's flanks. Behind him his wife limped in rags.

'Where are you off to?' shouted the driver.

'To the hospital in Cetinje.'

'Are you ill, then?'

'No, not me. My wife.'

Everyone in the bus burst out laughing, and turning the driver said, 'There's a real Montenegrin for you.'

But when we reached the plateau the panorama of the fjord was swallowed up behind us, and we were surrounded by boundless expanses of grey stone and white snow-drifts. We passed a few houses; they were low and built of the same stone as the ground, and therefore seemed to have grown from the living rock. Everything had become poorer, bitterer, harsher, and it was here I could feel Italian Montenegro changing into Crnagora, which also means 'black mountain', but has a more austere ring, like that of steel on stone. And over all, Lovćen. A king in his rosy mantle of snow, witness to all that is Crnagora — all the bloody battles, all the hubris, its barren stone notwithstanding.

The bus halted at one such stone village. Near it, Lovćen hurled its summit to the sky, pale green in the dusk. There was a frozen sub-post-office on the upper floor of the only two-storeyed house, and on the ground floor a tavern where the only heating was that of plum brandy. The village is called Njegoš and is the birthplace of Petar Njegoš of the Petrović dynasty.

He has been compared to David. Unaware of the Goliath he was to encounter, he herded sheep on the slopes of the mountain he made his own; yet with every conquest he became more lost, more Lovćen itself. Much later he sang the praise of Lovćen in a poem of which there is a sixty-year-old Swedish translation.

Giant Lovćen, high thy head is lifted,
mighty above the clouds thy rugged crown,
looking in majesty upon the world
of wonders lying scattered at thy feet:
The rock, the bloodsplashed rock of Crnagora,
Bosnia's land, Albania's, ever stern;
the Turkish inland plains, the Latin coasts.
 Into thy lap a thousand centuries
have hurled their thunders, as a man may toss
an apple to the apron of a maid.
 All life thou spurnest from thee, save alone
the life that is the eagle's, or the wolf's –
the valiant Miloš, noble Karadjordje –
and spew'st the gall of thy anathema
upon the race of the betrayer, Vuk.

At the end of the nineteenth century Alfred Jensen, who translated the poem, was awarded second prize by the Swedish Academy for his rendering of Njegoš's main work, the lyrical verse-drama *Gorski Vijenac* (The Mountain Wreath). Unlike Petar Njegoš, Alfred Jensen is better known abroad than in his own country; he was perhaps our greatest Slavonic scholar, and his monograph on *Osman* and its author the seventeenth century poet Ivan Gundulić of Dubrovnik opened the way for research into early Croat literature. In Njegoš's castle at Cetinje, now a museum, there are editions of *Gorski Vijenac* in fifty other languages, but the Swedish version is the exotic jewel of the collection.

'The Yugoslav minister in Stockholm sent it to us,' said Professor Ivan Vukmanović, the curator of the Njegoš collection. 'He came upon it quite by chance in an antique shop.'

Gorski Vijenac is a true national epos, glowing with heroic, Byronic romance in its descriptions of mighty battles with the Turks in by-gone times. The fight for freedom – the fighting itself – was as necessary to the Montenegrins as eating, sleeping and making love. After the battle of Kossovo, when the Turks won dominion over large areas of the Balkans, Montenegro, like Dubrovnik, succeeded in preserving its independence; unlike Dubrovnik it did this not by means of the tongue but by force of arms and by constantly staining the rocks with its blood. It is indeed from the dried blood on the hills, says legend, that Crnagora-Montenegro won its name.

But the Vladika, its ruler, had not only to do battle with invaders from without, but also with his own rebellious chieftains. Many tribes had been forced to adopt the Moslem faith, while others had done so voluntarily; and the people had a perpetual thirst for blood and a longing to try their strength. Njegoš confesses his despair: 'If I seek to maintain peace, the people say they have a weak prince and sing the praises of former heroes. If I court war, they long for the days when peace prevailed in the land. If I impose taxes to finance the war against the Turks, my people say they would rather pay the money to the Turks to leave them in peace.' To be ruler of such a people and of a land that is mostly rock, bitter in winter and an anvil under the heat of summer, was indeed the harshest of destinies.

Montenegro's government was a theocracy. Political and religious power was gathered into one hand: that of the Vladika. The Vladika had to be celibate, therefore the position was not hereditary. By custom he chose some relative to be his successor, and usually the choice fell upon a nephew. Since the eighteenth century, power had passed from uncle to nephew through the Petrović-Njegoš dynasty. The last Vladika was the poet-prince Petar II Njegoš; after his time the supreme office was secularized.

One summer day in 1830 the shepherd boy Rade Njegoš became Vladika in Cetinje. His uncle Petar I, then 83, had been ruling for forty-six years. Rebellion had broken out among the clans, and the chieftains were summoned to Cetinje to compose their quarrels. It was then that the old Vladika had a stroke. He was carried dying into his house, where he appointed the seventeen-year-old Rade as his successor. Rade looked round: all about him the chieftains were standing with loaded rifles. In an instant of prophetic terror he sensed the life that awaited him, the responsibility for this untamed mountain race that demanded all and gave so little in return — the huge burden that was being laid upon his shoulders. He wept in his fear, and not until he had been dragged by force into the monastery did he take the oath of succession.

The weeping boy became a many-sided genius condemned to a

microcosmos; confined to too small a language in too small a country. There he sat in his mountain domain which meant nothing to the rest of Europe, yet which made him feel as if he were bearing the burdens of the whole world. He would have liked best to throw off these obligations — the obligation to abstain from love, to fight against Allah, to mediate between chieftains, to sacrifice himself for his people. His life was a tense drama — a battle between internal and external forces that were constantly at variance with one another. He was a Hamlet forced into action. He was a dual man, his own David, his own Saul, the doubter and consoler. Outwardly he was learned and wise, accustomed to moving about the great cities of Europe, such as St Petersburg and Rome; inwardly he was a self-taught man who had to build up his own image of the universe, his own philosophy, stone by stone; with Lovćen, the rock of his childhood, as its centre. Outwardly he was a giant, who might have slain a Turk with one blow of his fist; yet in the mornings he spat blood on to his pillow. He united Crnagora and chased the Crescent from the sky of Montenegro. He wrote poems as enduring as Lovćen itself, but came home from Italy to die. He came back to the country that was his burden, heavier than all the rock that was Crnagora — to die there. His companions in the boat noticed that he wept when he saw Lovćen.

Laborious travellers of the nineteenth century have remarked on the startling experience of descending from these wild hills with their wild clansmen to a plain encircled by a jagged skyline, of finding on this plain a castle and in this castle a billiard-playing prince; a giant over six foot eight who exchanged the billiard-cue for a bishop's crozier, the crozier for a sword, the sword for the poet's pen; a leader of Church and Army who was at the same time the greatest romantic poet to write in the Serbo-Croat language.

But Montenegro is a small country, beyond our knowledge, outside our hearts. The Light of Microcosmos does not extend beyond its borders.

Petar II Njegoš, whom the gods loved, died at the age of thirty-

Svetji Stefan, off the coast of Montenegro. It is to be turned into a dollar-earning hotel.

Sarajevo: the Bazaar.

eight. His burial-chapel was built on the summit of Lovćen. His desire to sleep among the eagles was no Byronic affectation; it was a natural resting-place for him, a transition as natural as ours when we are buried, and melt into the soil that was once our field. No prince ever had such a resting-place, or one loftier, nearer to the voice of the winds. Here his spirit watched over the realm he had fought for, suffered for and sung.

Njegoš was no superficial traveller. He made his great journey within the little world which was an insignificant pile of rocks in our universe. The storms of Microcosmos filled his chapel with snow. This hill was no more than a dwarf among the full-grown mountains, but above it were all the sparkling eyes of the firmament.

In that night of stars the snow, pale and blue, crunched beneath my shoes. To think that not so many miles from Cetinje, palms grew by the warm city-wall of Kotor! This was no sweet-smelling night, but a night of whetted crystal. The moon shed its white chill over the houses. The serpentine road that had twisted its way up from Boka Kotorska became the main street of Cetinje, broad and tree-lined; then vanished in the darkness, and divided. One arm led to Titograd, the new capital which in Cetinje is called contemptuously the gold-diggers' camp, and the other down to Budva on the coast.

When I woke next morning the ten thousand people of Cetinje were already up. The Grand Hotel had its back to the sun, but the light washed the earth street with cool silver. From my window I could see that I had lost the south – lost not only the almond-blossom but also the chalk-white cubes of Dubrovnik, the loggias of Hvar, the sun-cleansed quay of Cavtat. The wide main street, the blue or pink-washed walls of low houses under pitched roofs, the open spaces – it was a return to the north. Cetinje was different, very different from the towns of the south with their sun-choked alleys, their tightly-packed, timorous houses, in a light knowing no gradation between dazzling white and the black purple of the shadows. Cetinje was a rolled-out town – or peasant village – in pale pastel, open to the pilot-light of the winter sun. And in summer, in what a fiery ague must those rocks quiver! No tower, no campanile competed with the snow-flecked ring of mountains round the plateau. Even the chapel, enclosed by a railing made of thousands of rifle-barrels taken from defeated Turks, crouched between two Bogomili tombstones. Even Njegoš's castle Biljarda, named after the billiard-table which was a present from the Czar and which had been carried up the donkey-trails from Kotor by the strongest men in Crnagora, was a humble building close to the ground. The Vladika's Orthodox monastery was as grey as the rock it grew from. Cetinje was a princely peasant village. In fits of melancholy Njegoš used to say, 'I am a prince among barbarians and a barbarian among princes.'

Njegoš was succeeded by his nephew Danilo, but in 1860 Danilo was assassinated down in Kotor, and it was his nephew Nikita who plucked the fruit from the tree of the great Njegoš.

Nikita too was of Njegoš blood, and was a poet and a warrior. The uncle of Petar II Njegoš, Petar I, had improvised lyrical pieces to the music of the *gusle*. But he was unschooled and illiterate, so that his songs had to be noted down by others. As in too warm a spring, his flowering was profuse but brief. Njegoš brought the art to perfection, but with Nikita the princely poetry – and the princely state – had lost its primeval freshness and the rough power ennobled by Njegoš. The work of the one was born of a deep affinity with land and people, while the other had to create a décor in which to weep and sing. At Njegoš's graveside, tears flowed from his pen.

His lyrical art thinned as his belly thickened, and as time went on he became more and more of a musical comedy king. He defeated the Turks and the victorious banner of Montenegro was hoisted at Scutari during the Balkan war of 1918. But although Nikita cele-brated his fiftieth year of rule by proclaiming Montenegro a king-dom, his star was declining. In the Parisian *demi-monde* his son, the Crown Prince Danilo, was busy disgracing himself, and like the Danilo of the Merry Widow he passed into the next world singing,

'*Da geh' ich zu Maxim, dort bin ich so intim*. . . .' After some manoeuvring during the first world war, Nikita was deposed in November 1918 and had to fly to the Riviera, which had always been his spiritual home. He died in Cannes in 1921 and is buried at San Remo.

A museum is at its best when it ceases to be one. Such was Nikita's little palace: a modest two-storeyed house with a mezzanine floor on which was the library. The door leading from the hall on the left opened straight into his secretariat, from whose windows he could watch his subjects passing to and fro on the unpaved square: members of parliament, ministers and all the poor Montenegrins. Hunched shadows, women with shawls pressed to their withered mouths, soldiers – and what giants they were – with red breeches, shining buttons and a broad sash in which were thrust three or four silver-mounted pistols.

There was the writing-desk, the pen, and the cup containing green glass balls. Had these balls had time to soak up the ink of the last signature? Was the sovereign merely on tour and expected back any day? Were the queen, the princes and princesses on a trip to Kotor? The envoys playing preference somewhere, leaving the rooms to their venetian-blinded after-dinner nap?

Mirko Jovanović, Partisan and now interpreter for foreign visitors to Cetinje, showed me the upper floor, where the private apartments and the reception-rooms were. Externally Nikola's residence looked more like a manor-house than a palace; internally more the home of a patrician family than that of royalty.

'Here,' said Mirko Jovanović, 'was the foreign envoys' dining-room, and this was Nikita's audience-chamber. The king slept here and the queen here. This room belonged to the beautiful Elene who was to marry Vittorio Emmanuele of Italy. Liszt played on that piano!'

What gorgeous tastelessness! What a hotch-potch of plush, furniture and china! French Empire . . . Venetian chairs . . . the Indonesian room . . . Dresden dinner-service, Japanese jars and Greek

vases. Persian rugs, Italian silk shawls, Montenegrin blankets. . . .
The walls were an Almanach de Gotha of royal and ducal relations
in oils and silhouettes — and there was a photograph of Queen Vic-
toria, with a signed greeting in her own hand. There was the cabinet
of Orders, displaying the Order of the Elephant, the Russian Order
of St Andrew, the Order of the Garter. . . .

It was the period of our grandfathers carried to extremes. An opti-
mistic period which at once encouraged a new machine-made world
and sought to hold open the door to the past. A period intoxicated
by the snorting speed of the steam locomotive, marking the transition
to the world of the sound barrier and the atomic bomb; which in
turn is just a further step towards a world wherein the conquest of
the sound-barrier will seem no more than the movement of snails
between atomic mushrooms. And here in Montenegro there were
neither steam locomotives nor machinery; nothing but the attempt
to seem what the great world was.

Here they had cut the navel-cord linking them with the past – the
past of *gusle* and donkey – yet feared to live by the precepts of machinery. Nikita was a period prince; he strayed among dead epochs,
incapable of making friends with the new forces which he fancied he
could control. He found one setting for himself in Victorian morality,
another in an exotic gift from India, a third by Njegoš's grave. He
complicated, multiplied his existence. He filled his house and his life
with objects *ad nauseam*. He created a kingdom without cohesion,
even within the wreath of Montenegro, and proclaimed himself king
– a smug and bloated king – of Crnagora, all unaware that he was
drifting into a pent-up chaos which, if a single crack appeared in the
dam, must break forth in deluge. In these brittle rooms, still warm
from Nikita's breath, unconsciousness of disaster was so deep as to be
a coma. A snap of the fingers and the palace would have collapsed.

Here in Nikita's residence, while the ruler was temporarily absent,
never to return, one felt that the shot fired not far away, in Sarajevo,
was necessary and sufficient to set the world ablaze. Nikita's palace
was a Microchaos, mirror of a greater chaos which burst forth in a

first world war. The Crnagora of 1900 had survived itself and must be dissolved.

The square before Nikita's palace is a panorama of epochs. There Njegoš's heroic Biljarda, here Nikita's miniature mansion; across the square a bone-coloured house where a child was born to the Karadjordje line — a child who was to become the despot Alexander II of Yugoslavia, and die from a bullet fired in Marseilles. It was of him that Tito said, 'He was a cruel man, an enemy of the people. But I can never accuse him of doing what King Peter did: of leaving his country in its hour of greatest peril — of forsaking his people when they stood in direst need of a leader. Nothing like that had ever happened before in the history of the Yugoslav people. I do not believe that Alexander would have done this. He never ran away. He was never a coward.'

'No, he was never a coward,' said Mirko Jovanović, to whose hands I had been entrusted. It was like an echo of Tito. But Mirko Jovanović was thin; he could not afford an opinion of his own, or new teeth to replace those that had rotted away in his upper jaw. Mirko Jovanović admired Tito more than anything in the world, and hated nothing so much as Stalin and the Pope. He talked of the gallantry of the army, he talked about the ravening wolves that snapped and slavered after Little Red-Riding-hood Yugoslavia. He had the same sort of falsetto voice as that of Zeljko Brihta in Zagreb, the young *Vjesnik*-journalist who had been my watchdog on the Stepinac visit. The difference was that whereas Brihta developed his game as a chess-champion does, with an infinite number of combinations, albeit confined within the limits of sixty-four black and white squares, Mirko Jovanović merely reproduced. A film rolled through his head and he was incapable of projecting any picture but the one that had been fed into him. This pleasant and benevolent Soviet-hater had been a pro-Soviet fanatic before 1948, and would still have been so today if the board of directors away up there in their inaccessible fastness had not given orders for a change of programme.

Above all, Mirko Jovanović was a Montenegrin. He was undismayed by the desolation of those hills, he did not see his own poverty, and for him the value of Boka Kotorska's beauty lay in the fact that it made foreigners giddy to look at it. Mirko Jovanović was a patriot; when he told of the heroism of the Partisans, those Partisans were Montenegrins.

'We have at least ten Montenegrins in the Yugoslav army,' he said. 'No one in the country can fight as we can.'

And this was no lie. Dapčević, the commander-in-chief, is a Montenegrin. The first in every clash, the bravest, the man readiest to sacrifice himself, is always a Montenegrin. For him it is a disgrace to come second; therefore a Montenegrin platoon does not number off 'one — two, one — two', but 'one — you-to-the-right-of-him; one — you-to-the-right-of-him'. While a young man from Dubrovnik will simulate every kind of disease when called up, a Montenegrin will weep if rejected. But he would rather not work. Fighting is not work; fighting is a noble craft bordering on art. A Montenegrin will do all he can to retire early in life, so that he may sit on the steps in the sun talking of distant battles and tearing open the memory of old wounds.

Such a man was Mirko Jovanović.

He was loyal and hungry for knowledge, and he learned easily. His enthusiasm was quickly kindled and he was conservative in his faith in Socialism and Tito. In short he was a Montenegrin. And it is of Montenegrins that anecdotes are told throughout the country.

'There's a lot of nonsense talked about us,' said Mirko Jovanović. 'Not a tenth part of it is true.'

We walked down the main street. Although the ground was soft and slushy, and squelched round their shoes, the population of Cetinje were strolling up and down beneath the grudging afternoon sun to get up an appetite. A fussy-looking little man flitted about like a moth, his pocket full of stencilled notices which he handed out to those he met:

'Ah, Mr Minister — a meeting at seven o'clock this evening, to discuss the sanitary conditions in the high school. Ah, Mr Secretary of State, how fortunate! The minister will be present at seven o'clock this evening ... a meeting about the insanitary conditions at the high school. Why, good day, Councillor; yes, this evening. ... '

The little man ran bowing on his way, summoning one dignitary after another to the meeting: exalted comrades, strolling in dignity between the puddles, with pointed white moustaches and round bellies; such for instance was the Minister of Health, a former jobbing painter of Cetinje.

'There are only a few ministries left here now,' said Mirko Jovanović. 'Cetinje is the shadow of what it was in the first war. Titograd grabs everything; president, ministers. ... It makes one feel unwanted. But on the other hand Cetinje is becoming more and more of a cultural centre. Montenegro's only daily newspaper is published here, and we have faculties and high schools. And did you know that it was in Montenegro that the art of printing was invented? Before Gutenberg's day there were monks in the neighbouring monastery who printed books with movable type.'

The western range drove its jagged points into the sun, and the hollow in which Cetinje lay was filled with the blood of dusk. We passed a building which looked far more like a princely home than did Nikita's.

'That house was once a capitalist bank. It looks like it, doesn't it? The Germans blew it up when they retreated, but we rebuilt it with our own hands, by voluntary labour; and now it's used by the Intellectual Workers' Club.'

'Then I've come to the right place,' I said. 'I have a letter to the director of the art gallery, Milos Vušković.'

'He usually looks in there about this time.'

'Will you come?'

Mirko Jovanović made a gesture of deprecation.

'No, no — I don't fit in there. I'm not the right sort. You see, I really live in a very small way; we have only one room at home, and that has to do for everything. In the daytime we call it the living-room; when we cook we call it the kitchen; at night it's our bedroom; and when we're eating it's the dining-room. And it's a nursery for most of the twenty-four hours. There are six of us and we sleep in pairs. Father sleeps with little Jovan — he's only four. I sleep with my wife. We have two chairs and we put them together for our two oldest children. You see I'm a poor man. This club is too grand for me.'

I walked up the steps alone, and alone I entered a huge room, big enough for ice-hockey. The ceiling was supported by pillars, and two bloated Japanese vases dozed against them. Symmetrically arranged for inspection, like troops drawn up on parade, stood little groups of armchairs and tables. Along the walls were glass cases full of precious china. Two chess-players sat at one end of the room; there was time for one of them to make a move before the click of the last piece reached the other end. It was a vast room, and there was a hollow ring about it which enhanced its emptiness. Then I discovered some elderly men sitting slumped and silent round a table behind one of the pillars.

I found the man I was looking for at once, from the description that had been given me in Dubrovnik. He had a big black moustache which stuck out far beyond his cheeks and which he stroked unceasingly — not without pride. His brown eyes were sunk behind the high pads of fat on his cheekbones. He might have been handsome, but he wasn't — he only thought so. This was the director of the art gallery of Cetinje, Milos Vušković.

'A Swede!' he cried, throwing out his arms. 'I'm delighted to see you. Welcome, welcome!' A sentimental note came into his voice: 'Sweden, Sweden! What memories are stirred within my breast. Anders Zorn, Bruno Liljefors, Carl Larsson! Are they still alive?'

I regretted that they were all dead.

'Ah, I wonder whether my wife is living. I was married to a Swede — ah, but it was long ago. She vanished from my world and I'm once more in the Cetinje of my childhood. At one time – this was

Mostar. A town in picturesque decay.

Sarajevo: the corner where the shot was fired.

From my hotel window I could see eighteen big mosques. (*Below*) Tombstones
on the slopes above Sarajevo.

There were ways of dodging the no-veil law. (Below) On Wednesdays the peasants came down from the hills to sell their produce.

before the war – I ran a satirical little newspaper in Belgrade. I toiled day and night while life slipped past me, without trace. ... ' (He stroked his moustache.) 'One day I woke and said, "What are you doing with your life, Milos Vušković?" On that day I began to live. I became a drawing-master — a common or garden drawing-master. And look at me now! The director of the Cetinje art gallery! My people need me, you understand — my people need me. But allow me to introduce my friends. The painter Alexander Prijić, director of the Liberation Museum. Veljko Milatović, director of *Pobjeda*, our daily newspaper. Doctor Niko Lazarević, one of Yugoslavia's most eminent radiologists. And now you must taste our speciality: *kaimak*, ewe's-milk cheese. Waiter! Bread, *kaimak* and wine!'

With Dr Lazarević I talked socialized health-service:

'What do I want with huge fees?' said Dr Lazarević. 'I have my house and my hospital, and the State takes care of the rest.'

With Alexander Prijić I talked art:

'If you'll come to the gallery tomorrow,' said the director of the Liberation Museum, 'I will show you our treasures, among other things a picture of the oldest olive-tree in Europe — over three thousand years old. But we have also many good modern painters in Cetinje. Milutinović, for instance, and Petar Lubarda, who did that magnificent painting on the wall.'

The magnificent painting on the wall was a canvas suffering from elephantiasis; an immense picture-postcard of voluntary railway-workers, carried out in a sort of socialist-realist impressionism.

'He's gone abstract now,' said Prijić. 'He doesn't believe in this sort of thing any more. But wait; in a year he'll have come back to Art. Mark my words. You shall have an introduction to him. Go and see him when you get to Belgrade.'

But with the director of the Montenegrin daily paper I did not talk; he sat silent and looked at his shoes.

'He's thinking of the Nikšić of his childhood and the Belgrade of his student years,' remarked the director of the gallery.

'It's seven o'clock,' said the director of *Pobjeda*, raising his sad face

with the sadly shining eyes. 'Excuse me, but my minister's waiting.'
He crossed the room with soft steps.

The director of the gallery:

'I must say goodbye to my minister; he leaves for Titograd in a quarter of an hour.'

Dr Niko Lazarević:

'My minister—'

'Forgive me, but how can an ex-painter be expert in the care of the sick?' I asked.

The doctor had already risen to follow the others out; his voice was half superior, half irritated as he replied:

'But my dear sir — don't you know? That man was one of our greatest Partisans!'

So they all disappeared and I remained behind with my *kaimak*, my brown bread and my red wine. The ministers had assumed charge of these eminent men of Montenegro; and the men flaunted their ministers as a cock flaunts its comb. Mysteriously, as if controlling the destinies of the world, they sped away with the magic word 'minister', like a talisman, on their lips. Such was the palace of the intellectual directors of Cetinje. Perhaps the light of Microcosmos had not quite faded from Crnagora and its 600,000 Montenegrins. Perhaps a ray or two, like the X-rays of Dr Lazarević, penetrated into that great room in the nationalized palace of capitalist bankers.

But when next day I was waiting for the bus that was to take me to Budva, down on the coast, I noticed a white-haired man wearing the flat fez which is customary in Montenegro. He was sitting on the steps of the Orthodox monastery where Njegoš, the great Njegoš, wept like the child he was when forced to swear the oath to his people. He sat there reading the paper, and a crystal drop reflected Cetinje in his moustache.

'Montenegro is finished,' he said. 'I'm an old nationalist, sir, yes. I fought at Scutari.'

He rose, and his gout creaked.

'Yes, sir' (and with every 'sir' he bowed). 'Life is hard for us true Montenegrins.'

Then I saw that the crystal drop on the rheumatic warrior's moustache had fallen not from his nose but from his eyes.

We who were bound for Budva were waiting outside the bus-office when the man in charge came out and counted us.

'Only ten of you,' he said. 'It's not worth getting out our fine great bus for that. Take a taxi.'

With that he went back and settled down to sleep.

We rushed to the taxi-station which boasted a single car: a once luxurious tourer dating from 1925. It had undoubtedly been a very splendid vehicle during the monarchy. It was a five-seater, but with the owner we were ten. And now began a journey which is a classic feature of every book about travel in primitive mountain countries, whether in Kabylie, Kilimandjaro or Sierra Nevada.

The driver, a man of seventy, swung the starting-handle. By all the rules the engine ought not to have fired, but it did. We rolled on our way, and by the time we had gone two miles we were out in the wilderness, where we had our first puncture. Patiently we sat while the driver jacked us up and changed the wheel. When we were ready to go the car wouldn't start.

'It's the ignition,' said the driver, diving under the bonnet.

Two elderly peasant-women got out and squatted behind a bush. Another woman produced the classic fried chicken and shared it out among us. A gigantic Turk, who took up enough room for three, ate for four.

Suddenly the engine started; no one knew why. We crowded up together. On our left was a precipice and the road grew narrower and narrower. A guard-rail would have been quite out of keeping. Far down in the hollows I saw roofless villages that had been ripped open by Germans or Partisans.

Two new passengers joined us; there were now twelve of us, besides the fleas which had begun their lunch. The woman in the front seat covered the floor with her TB.

Now came the truly classic incident: the car stopped for the second time. Whatever may have been under the bonnet remained as silent as the tomb, and we stood immovably on the brink of a three-hundred-foot drop.

'The ignition's packed up again,' said the owner, and he got out. We waited as patiently as donkeys, and took the opportunity of scratching, now that the bumping of the car did not spoil our aim. The driver dashed between starting-handle, engine and driving-seat, rolling his eyes; nothing else moved.

'Perhaps we're out of petrol,' someone suggested thoughtlessly. This annoyed him.

'Do you think she runs on petrol? It's been paraffin since 1932. Why should it fail now?'

But the car was not to be bribed. We had now reached the stage at which the rules recommend a general consultation. One person suggested that we should wait until another car came, and get a tow; but the driver told us that only one car a day came this way. Another proposal was that we should telephone for a mechanic to come out from Cetinje; but there was no telephone nearer than Budva, which was still many miles away. At last the following suggestion prevailed: that we should push the car for another mile or two, to where the road began to run downhill; from there we could free-wheel to the coast. We started shoving, and with the united strength of eleven men we crawled slowly forward. After two hours of this we were on the point of giving up when the driver cried:

'Hell and damnation — she's in second; why the devil couldn't you say so?'

On we went with gritted teeth, and then, as we sweated and swore, the sky opened out before us; below lay the sea, like a silver shark, and the road dropped down among olive-groves and vineyards.

'There's my lovely Budva,' said the taxi-man.

And we saw Budva washing her hair in the water. We saw broad, golden-brown beaches like fallen autumn leaves beside the white curves of the breakers. It was spring. Slowly the car began to run downhill; we scrambled up on to the running-board and fell into our seats. Our silent engine accelerated and with every bend the speed increased. The driver sang, and turned round to us:

'—and there are no brakes. The last I remember of them was in the spring of 1928—'

Impetus carried us a mile or so along the edge of the shore as far as Budva. As the car rolled to a standstill came the classic finale: the engine started up of itself.

'What did I tell you?' said the driver. 'There was paraffin in her. Thought I was lying, didn't you?'

The Grand Hotel Avala, an overgrown sugar-lump tossed on to the beach without relevance to town or scenery, was as empty as a church. It had been built shortly before the war. When the foundations were dug, the soil was dumped in the sea, but children playing on the beach found objects of gold dating from the time when Budva was a Greek and then a Roman city. Hopeful treasure-seekers still come every summer to sift the wet sand through their fingers. Archaeologists have uncovered a Roman burial-ground behind the hotel, and are to dig down another sixty feet. Every foot is a layer of classical history.

The Hotel Avala was built for the Belgrade society of the monarchy, only six or seven miles from Alexander's summer palace at Miločer. But on this March day of sun and spring and summer I was the only guest. The waiter had once been a lawyer and studied at the Sorbonne and in Berlin, but later fell foul of the régime. Since his term of imprisonment he had assumed an enigmatic socialist mask. He spoke French like a taxi-driver of the sixteenth arrondissement and German like a barber of the Potzdamerplatz. And now Saturday evening was closing in and the Women's Anti-Fascist Union was to celebrate its anniversary with a display of Montenegrin folk-dancing. The dining-room, which was the size of a tennis-court, could, by movable glass walls, be united with the sea.

But Budva itself, like all these towns on the Adriatic coast, was dreamlike and mysterious. Like Dubrovnik it was built on a cliff with a massive wall snaking round it, but it was more lifeless, more desolate. In common with Hvar and Trogir it had the sea and the moon, but the wind that swept through the streets was as acrid as the smell of corpses in Boka Kotorska. Such was Budva, a town still in its death-throes. A waiting hotel on an evening in March. I was the only guest, the only foreigner. The stillness of the air had given place to the cold *bora*. The glass walls overlooking the sea were hauled up and a ray of sound shot out into the night, to be thrashed into resonant foam over the black shining rocks, and sink in the backwash of a receding breaker.

I began to long for Dubrovnik.

But Montenegro was not yet a finished chapter. There remained Miločer and Svetji Stefan, the Mont Saint Michel of the Adriatic, six miles south of Budva. The gates of Miločer – once the royal family's summer palace, now a recreation home for workers – stood open.

'For workers? For the big Party boys, you mean,' said the donkey-driver. 'Go on in. It's like another world.'

Behind thick hedges stood the villas of the staff. Oranges gleamed on the trees. The donkey-track through the village changed at the gates to an asphalt road, and passed the palace in a graceful arc. One's footsteps grew springier. Encircled by rocks, and by lawns that must once have been softer than rain, the Persil-washed mansion slept its winter sleep behind closed, chlorophyll-green shutters. Yes, it was another world, an isolated Eden; so different, that the things I had seen a few minutes before became part of a distant past, with all threads cut between it and the present: such things as the village shop and the post-office, where the peasants from the mountain hamlets who had come down to the coast to work sat babbling and befuddled at noon.

But beyond the cliff to the south the scene changed. There floated the island of Svetji Stefan: a pink foetus in blue water. A navel-cord of concrete connected the island with a beach of coarse sand. Seen from the olive-groves above, Svetji Stefan was the place of our secret dreams; an Atlantis which, loosed from the depths, had floated to the shore. It grew up like a coral reef and at its summit the white church gleamed like a lily. This is the prototype of Budva, of Dubrovnik.

Dear Svetji Stefan,

Patron of all hanged pirates, have you forsaken your city, that has hunched its back against the autumn gales of centuries? When was the cry of its last new-born baby heard? I send you this report from the coast of Montenegro; your fifteen poor families await the release of death. Hens seek their eggs in your scalped houses and your mill has broken its millstone heart. In your wind-fretted church an old woman in a kerchief mumbles prayers that no one understands; in the chapel beside the church Italians have poked loopholes in the walls and scrawled *Il Duce* above the altar.

Do you know that your city is to be turned into a luxury hotel? It will be one of the most fashionable in the world. When I walked up to the church, Branko Bon was there with the plans. The houses are to be restored, WCs will swish, the tunnel-arches will have red, in-direct lighting and the terraces will be enlarged into romantic places from which to view the sea under its moon. Branko Bon declares there's not much else one can do to save your pirates' stronghold. In itself, Svetji Stefan has nothing but curiosity value, he says. Wouldn't you rather your island weathered away and sank into the sea? I only ask; I make no comment.

Or have you become a hotel-magnate? Do you move in American circles and frequent the salons of Paris? 'I had my little yacht here before the war,' said Branko Bon, pointing out to sea; and he offered me a cigarette from a gold case, a gift from Tito. 'Perhaps it's a shame to do this to Svetji Stefan, but ours is a poor country and we need money.' Parked up at Miločer was Branko Bon's official car: a sky-blue Hillman sports model. 'Aren't my people wonderful?' he said.

'They give me a car, and no ordinary car, but a convertible fitted with radio.' Branko Bon is Tito's personal architect, and in case you should have the wrong idea about him I assure you without irony that he's a very agreeable and helpful man, and as far as I can judge an extremely good architect.

But I came to the island at an unfortunate moment. Branko Bon had with him a hundred workmen in grey, flimsy clothes and with hoods on their shaven heads: workmen not intended to be exhibited to foreigners. Who could guess that a foreigner would come here on a day in March, several months before the season opened? These grey men were the new inhabitants of the town; their listless moustaches and thin arms dangled limply over their plates. There was one man whom I called 'Tommy-gun' because he never said anything, but just waved the gun. With one of these signs he gave the order to fall in, and the hundred men disappeared with their picks and mattocks through the gate of the town, where a rosy-cheeked soldier with a flaxen fringe was waiting with *his* tommy-gun. 'These are all criminal convicts,' said Branko Bon. I had suspected nothing else.

I'm sure if you came here this summer disguised as a tourist, to inspect your town, your eyes would not be offended by these grey-clad criminals. They will be toiling somewhere else by then — perhaps in the mountains, building roads and widening the railway from Sarajevo to Dubrovnik.

For the present there's nothing more to tell you about your city, Svetji Stefan.

Yours,
T. S.

Night came, and day. Njegoš's Lovćen, hidden from Budva's eyes, was lit by the sun of Microcosmos. Warmth licked the sands, light sharpened the rocks, the swords of the cactuses flashed. The stones at the white rim of the sea had been polished to satin-shelled eggs. The first bathe of spring was salt and cold, and an old woman gathering firewood fled from the madman in the water.

The houses on the hillsides and the bazaars in the town showed that Turkey has
not lost its hold on Sarajevo.

Bosnian boy. His haircut shows him to be a Moslem.

Budva might have become a new Hvar, but Hvar had come first and nothing can repeat itself or be what it once was. One morning the waiter in Budva waved with his front tooth and a much-used handkerchief, and led me to the coasting-steamer *Gradac* bound for Dubrovnik. Seasick from her own rolling she vomited soot. Black smoke covered Budva and then the coast — Montenegro's coast. At last it quenched the sun that was Luča Mikrokosma.

11. SARAJEVO FROM ABOVE

IT hurt to leave Dubrovnik.
On the day before I went, Pero Lujak put his very soul
into a gala dinner.
There followed an evening full of farewell.

Next morning Putnik's grandest car – a Buick – was waiting in front
of the cathedral. The radio was switched on and we glided down to
Gruž. There lay the station, a bed-bug's paradise. The narrow-gauge
railway to Sarajevo — what a relic of Austrian times, with its toy
engine and carriages; the very sweepings under the seats were those
of the last century. Everything was dirty and sooty and narrow-
gauge — and off we chuffed with an engine at each end.

Farewell, sleeping Dubrovnik.

Farewell, Ombla, glimpsed through the smoke; the river, breaking
forth into daylight, the cypresses, the church of Prijevor and the
wine-casks of Komolac!

From Metković the train follows the valley of the River Neretva.
Six thousand feet of mountain fall sheer to the railway. The two little
breathless locomotives transmitted their joltings through the line of
coaches. At one place, at the foot of a tremendous hill, a rack-rail
engine was waiting to haul us up.

The bridge over the Neretva was my only reason for stopping at
Mostar, but it was reason enough. It's called the Roman bridge,
though it was built only a hundred years before the Turks left Mostar.
It spans the river like a drawn bow. To the steep shores cling lime-
washed houses that have black roofs like Chinese hats. I had left the
coast and Italy an afternoon ago, and come to Bosnia and Turkey.

There was a minaret at the top of the hill and yet my view of it was under the bridge. But a dumb minaret, a minaret without muezzin. Mostar, famed for its tobacco; a town of silent minarets and deserted mosques.

Mostar — the decay of Islam.

The river overflowed its banks. It was in spring spate — a spate of diluted yellow mud. Trees stuck their necks out of the water and stood swaying, like green giraffes in the savannahs. What a Turkish bath! The thermometer outside the optician's opposite the Hotel Neretva was panting at eighty-four in the shade.

A dazzling white April day in the town of solid-frozen winters and red-hot summers — Mostar.

Evening lit lamps on the verandah of the café above the river; it hung purple veils in the park in front of the hotel, and draped with mourning crêpe the monument to fallen Partisans.

All night the Neretva sang, and at dawn a grey centipede marched over the bridge to the station, waking me with its battle-songs. And at the station women crouched behind their bast baskets, waiting with the patience of angels for the barriers to open.

Preserve me from living in Mostar.

I left Mostar without regret.

The second day in Bosnia was the day of the poisonous tunnels. Two soldiers lay stretched out on the wooden benches of the compartment, and in the darkness of the tunnels they coughed and wept.

At Jablanica with its great power-station we left the Neretva and the new river now flowing alongside us was the Miljacka; the river of Sarajevo.

So I came to Sarajevo; and why does one come to Sarajevo if not to listen to the echo of a shot? But to see it one must climb up the hills to the south, for Sarajevo lies at the bottom of a bowl. In the daytime these heights shimmer palely green, sprinkled with white cubes of houses under black Chinese hats. Green and white are the colours of Sarajevo; sunlight swills over the slopes and washes the blossoming apple-trees.

Sit high up there while women in kerchiefs and baggy satin trousers trip by with their sad donkeys — sit and behold the town. A town enveloped in a light that clearly, transparently dissolves all details into tiny grains of dust. Sit here with your back against a rocking, turban-crowned tombstone. For everywhere, on every patch of grass, by every miry road where waters flashing in the sun ripple down towards the town, and along the bank of every ditch, these white stones stand in their hundreds, their thousands. Yes, the slopes round Sarajevo are one vast graveyard full of tombstones, like daisied meadows. The names of those sleeping beneath the stones have mouldered and the stones themselves are without inscriptions, without guardians and without the austere chill of Dalmatian burial-grounds: those strongrooms of the dead, amid the cool whisper of cypress. . . .

Sit here high above the town where the air is thin, and count tombstones as the sleepless count sheep. . . . Or attempt an equally hopeless task: count the mosques and minarets. They are as numberless as the stars, and from my hotel window alone I could count eighteen mosques. From my observation-post up here it was easy to pick out the Hotel Europa, that dark, Franz Joseph hotel where all foreigners are herded together: Americans on their way through from Belgrade, Swiss diplomats bound for Dubrovnik. The Hotel Europa, with its café and its dining-room with the mezzanine balcony for intrigues; the hotel which every evening watched my friend the press-artist Ali Mulabegović and the film producer Fedar Hanžeković drinking themselves silly, while the orchestra on the platform in the corner sobbed a *cevdalinka* or *Sarajevo Divno Mjesto* — Sarajevo, Divine Place.

But I was looking for mosques, and first of all the one in the next block to my hotel, the biggest and most exciting of them all; the biggest indeed in all Europe. It was built by the Turkish General Gazi Husref-Beg, who was governor here at the beginning of the sixteenth century; he lies buried in the courtyard. And the Ali Pasha mosque of the same century, drowned in foliage, in the Maršala Tita Ulica, the main street. Or the Emperor mosque erected by Husref-Beg's predecessor, Isabeg Isaković, which means 'Governor Isa, Isaac's son', and also that apparently most private mosque which lay, between waking and dreaming, at my very feet, behind gates that have not been opened for several hundred years. For a goat, this mosque is the most interesting of them all, for the grass within the fence grows in fine, juicy tussocks.

Sarajevo is a peculiar town and not beautiful until one is above it, when all the incongruities that battle together below blend into a whole; and the feature not noticed when one is down there – the pure, fresh foliage – is seen thrusting up here and there, as the minarets thrust up their lances beside the domes of the mosques. In the centre of the town, existence is cleft in two: into Turkey and Europe; to the east the bazaar-quarter, to the west Austrian pastrycook-architecture, and, along the Maršala Tita, a tendency to functionalism. The place swarms with people; there are now 120,000 inhabitants compared with 80,000 before the war, and in Vojvode Stepa Obala, the street alongside the River Miljacka, I saw a red double-decker bus imported from England running westward towards Ilidza, the spa with the hot springs.

Two-thirds of the population are Moslems, but very few are strict; at any rate my friend Ali Mulabegović the press-artist was cheerfully indifferent to Mohammed, or he would hardly have got drunk every night at the Hotel Europa, having already absorbed a pint of *slivovica* and a quart of wine before he arrived there. But who in this place can keep to the rules now that polygamy is forbidden? (This is a purely practical measure, for what socialist Moslem is upper-class enough to keep more than one wife?) For the last three years women have been forbidden to go veiled, but down in the bazaars I saw them cheat the law with their kerchiefs.

Men already married polygamously may keep their pre-war wives, and I met a man who had three.

'They're shrews, all of them,' he said. 'Proper witches. Oh, if only that new law had been brought in earlier! Rather than stay at home

I go out into the streets and smoke my pipe. But now we'll have a real Turkish cake.'

We squeezed between the booths in the great bazaar-area which is called Bascarsija, through the street of the braid-makers, the street of the gunsmiths, the streets of the hatters, tinkers, wheelwrights and tinsmiths, between wine-casks and kegs of brandy, sacks of maize and smoking flour, where bearded men in tapering trousers snored and snuffled off their potations with their fezes perched like steamer-funnels on their foreheads.

At last we reached the pastrycook, who with the air of a high priest dipped two of his cakes in the sweetest of syrup.

'A real Turkish cake — mm, mmm!' said the man with the three wives.

The muezzin in the minaret built by Husref-Beg completed his chant towards Mecca, and after the cake we drank sweet coffee, and water out of glasses which in Bosnia are never washed; here the national disease is not tuberculosis, nor cancer, but syphilis.

But now I was sitting up here and looking down over Sarajevo. All that is Sarajevo lies on the north bank of the Miljacka — everything except the People's Parliament of the People's Republic of Bosnia and Herzegovina, which stands on this side of the river, along the Obala Pariske Kommune. But the Praesidium of the People's Republic is housed in a modern building of countless corridors, in the Maršala Tita. What is there not in Sarajevo! A new university with about five thousand students; an opera-company, a ballet, a symphony orchestra, and a film-company where the great Fedar Hanžeković creates his pictures. And a *Kazaliste* — a theatre; a People's Theatre! But it had the look of any other theatre fifty years old, and it peers askance at the Princip Bridge diagonally opposite.

Sarajevo is indeed a progressive town.

From up here — was it a block-buster that laid bare the area adjoining the market place of Bascarsije? No, that was just where the socialist cleaners-up and the prophets of hygiene got busy with their brooms. There it was that the Moslem caravanserai stood, one of the most precious buildings dating from the time of the Turks. And what were those insects crawling about the ruins? Only the workmen who are to rebuild it exactly as it was. . . .

Those dirty Turks. . . .

A stream runs through the bazaar. At the time when a piped water-supply had not yet been invented in Sarajevo, that stream was the street-cleaning system of the Bascarsija. Every afternoon the stream was dammed, potters and silversmiths put up their shutters and the water flushed the streets.

Now the streets are washed down every morning by fire-hoses.

On these mornings in the Hotel Europa, my alarm-clock, as in Mostar, was a grey centipede. The Yugoslav army marched at dawn, with rattling gun-carriages behind one-eyed tractors, with their steady tramp and their battle-songs: '*Živio Tito! Živio Tito plan!*' Only a few leaves of April were left in the calendar, and the First of May, *prvi maja*, cast its shadows before: the day of parades and demonstrations of power.

Outside the House of the Yugoslav Army – in the great square opposite the Roman Catholic cathedral – officer-cadets appeared in red, tapering breeches with stripes down the sides, black boots and cornflower-blue tunics. Inside, in the concert-hall, beneath Tito's portrait and the hammer and sickle, Sluzny the Polish-Belgian pianist was playing.

But here where the valley begins, the goat bleated and frolicked over consecrated ground. Oh, Sarajevo, divine town with your holy mosques and juicy grass! Sit up here above the valley and listen for the echo of a shot, looking therefore westward along the Miljacka. The swelling yellow Neretva is Mostar's river, but Sarajevo's is the dwindling Miljacka, and when it reaches the Princip bridge it takes on the colour of blood. The stones of the river bed thrust their red heads above the surface.

Franz Ferdinand, the heir to the throne, drove in his open carriage from the Town Hall, an Austrian imitation of Moorish style. Princip was waiting by the bridge. But that day the river ran high.

He fired his pistol, tore through the crowd, leaped into the water and swam sixty yards or so, to dive under the little bridge where the mountain stream joins the Miljacka. At that spot Gavrilo Princip was seized.

Now the corner house almost opposite the bridge has been turned into a museum. An American remarked:

'We hang men who murder our presidents. They're criminals for all time. Here they get to be national heroes.'

Far away to the north I could see a group of yellow buildings: the Sarajevo Museum. That alone could occupy a lifetime. But I came here for the echo of a shot, and in the ethnographical museum Professor Popović shook his head.

'Why should I tell you? You can ask me about anything else – about Bosnian peasants and national dress and jewellery – but not about that.'

Grey moustache and kindly smile — that was Professor Popović, the last survivor of the group of which Princip was the fanatical tool.

But the Sarajevo Museum. . . .

Let us begin with the time when our own country still lay in its deep-freeze, waiting to thaw into history.

As I said, it would take a lifetime in this well-ordered museum to survey some thousand years of Bosnian history; but who could not sit for a lifetime under a blossoming apple-tree, and never tire of looking down over Sarajevo? In the National Museum I found a man at a piano, and on the piano was a tape-recorder. This was Cvjetko Rihtman, collector of songs from Bosnian mountain villages. He was fully persuaded that these songs are the last relics of the aborigines of the western Balkans, the Illyrians; and he dreamed of a fantastic musical Kon-Tiki. For Professor Jaap Kunst of the *Koninklijk Instituut voor de Tropen* in Amsterdam had found the same music and the same instruments in Java, and a musical trail right through the continent as far as the western Balkans.

'You may be sure that Indonesian music – even the Indonesians themselves – originated with the Illyrians,' said Cvjetko Rihtman.

The taxis had seen their best days. (*Below*) The Maršala Tita, the main street of Belgrade, seen from my window in the Hotel Balkan. Note the traffic!

The Danube shore along the Iron Curtain — on the Yugoslav side.

She was from Niš, a town on the railway between Belgrade and Skoplje.

Surla-player from Rugova, near Albania.

'Those Illyrians who so mysteriously disappeared. They may have crossed the whole continent to Indonesia.'

He switched on his tape-recorder, but when I came out into the street and took the clattering tram into the town, the loudspeakers which had just been hung up in the trees began bellowing. They were bellowing Beethoven's Dead March and flags hung limply at half-mast. For three days the piano at the Hotel Europa remained locked and a thin gauze of black dust lay over the stage of the People's Theatre. For three days *Vjesnik*, the Zagreb newspaper, appeared with a black border and with five pages out of six devoted to obituary articles. In the office of *Oslobodjanje*, the local paper, the ping-pong table was put down in the cellar and the gigantic Mrs Seleš, temperamental director of the light music programmes of Radio Sarajevo, rolled her heavy body and flung out her hands:

'What a loss — what a calamity! Everything is upside down! Oh, oh!'

Rain over Sarajevo.

But who had died?

Boris Kidrić.

And who was Boris Kidrić?

But didn't I know? That was fantastic. Why, he was the man who had drawn up the new finance- and production-plan.

But the goat that jumped the fence rubbed itself against the mosque and munched sacred grass.

From this quiet place, an isle amid the white daisies of death, the Orthodox church at the eastern end of the Maršala Tita is out of sight. But he who has not sought out the black light, the black, smoked icons, the woodcarving and the black brass lamps, has never been in Sarajevo.

Sit above Europe and the Orient, above Mohammed and Christ and Tito, Turkey and Austria and Yugoslavia. See Sarajevo and hear the echo of a shot.

At the Hotel Europa, a hotel with a view of eighteen mosques, Ali Mulabegović was swilling *slivovica*.

'*Sarajevo divno mjesto* . . . Sarajevo, divine place.'

'Bloody orchestra,' he said, 'in a bloody town.'

But to see Sarajevo one must climb the hills to the south, for Sarajevo lies at the bottom of a bowl. In the daytime these heights shimmer palely green and are sprinkled with the white cubes of houses. Green and white are Sarajevo's colours. Light pours over the slopes and froths in the blossoming apple-trees.

But at night Sarajevo twinkles like a fallen firmament of stars.

12. BELGRADE DIARY

MAY DAY EVE. When I woke my head was hitting something hard, and saliva had run down on to my jacket from the left corner of my mouth. There was an acrid smell of soot, and something green and blurred was sweeping past my eyes. My left arm was still asleep. My wrist-watch was ticking on towards five, so I couldn't have been sleeping for more than an hour. My head bumped on the table flap and cards lay scattered on the floor. It was cold and my neck ached from the draught.

The green blur took shape but not outline. I looked for trees but there were none. I seemed to be crossing an Atlantic in a windless summer dawn. White ships glided past, and there were masts. But I saw low bridges and on the bridges carts with white horses and high, high wheels. Further off, moulded into statues, other carts approached; slowly, one by one, a whole caravan that did not end even at the horizon.

Outside the carriage-windows Serbia was waking up, just as I imagined Serbia would wake. Everything was changing. The white ships became long farm-buildings, the masts were poles carrying electric cables; the bridges over the water were roads and the dawn sea was a plain, horizonless Serbia. Only the horses and carts remained what they were. And still no trees.

It was now four months since I had arrived in Yugoslavia.

Belgrade station: the most wretched of any in the capitals of Europe — though I have never been in Tirana.

The morning sun swept the streets with its pale light and it was raining drearily. Porters fought over me, and a policeman rushed up:

'I speak German, English, French, Hungarian, Russian, Italian, Bulgarian and Polish. What can I do for you?'

'Call a taxi in Serbo-Croat.'

My hotel was called the Balkan and I had a view of a small park, where there were green poplars and lawns. Beyond this the town fell away towards a stretch of river. That must be the Sava. As evening fell I saw Tito's signature flash on in neon light, on the other side of the river.

I had arrived in Belgrade; and long though I may have postponed this arrival, Belgrade is necessary. A journey must not be confined to one through moods and feelings.

The feelings born of a sleepless night are strange. Seldom are we so near to ourselves — so near tears and a wonderful joy. We can analyse everything with the sharpness of broken glass. The simplest, most self-evident thoughts — how extraordinary that they should have lain dormant so long. And what extraordinary paradoxes, never ventured upon before.

But every second annihilates the last, and so it was on this Eve of May Day: every coming instant clear, every past one clouded.

From the hotel I went out into Belgrade and the air closed a grey helmet over my head. The broad streets were designed for heavy traffic, but I counted more point-duty policemen than cars. Most of these were marked CD: there were a few taxis, the rest was State transport. But there were trolley-buses and there were parks — green, well-tended parks. And there were barefooted begging children, always on the look-out for foreigners in the cafés.

From in front of the Parliament House in the Bulevard Revolucije, which after the war had been called the Boulevard of the Red Army, came the noise of hammering: the tribunes of honour for next morning's parade were going up. And in the Teracije, the central area just by the hotel, stood the Albania, Belgrade's white sky-scraper with its flat-iron façade. Over this was stretched a huge portrait of Tito, and the building was surmounted by a red neon star. The Trg Republike lay behind the Albania, and round the Trg Republike were the National Museum (a former bank), the National Theatre and at a little distance the House of the Yugoslav Army.

This evening the streets have been as shiny as patent leather. No neon lights were reflected in them. In a restaurant I found something costing seven dinars and I ordered five of it, and something else costing forty and I ordered one. It was as I'd been told: Serbian cooking falls little short of French. The dish that cost seven dinars was *ćevap-čići*, grilled meat-balls, and the one costing forty dinars was *ražnjići* — a piece of lean lamb roasted on a little spit. With it went shredded onion and red wine. It tasted heavenly.

But tomorrow I shall wake with the taste of onion in my mouth.

May Day. Rain, rain all day.

I had been advised to be out early if I wanted to see anything of the parade. Unfortunately I was too late to get a ticket to Tito's tribune of honour. The legation did what it could to arrange this, and so did the Press Club, but in vain.

Though it was barely a quarter past seven, thousands upon thousands of people were streaming up the Maršala Tita. The flags lining the route were drooping: the Communist banner and the Yugoslav flag, red, blue and white with a gilt-edged red star. Dejected, wretched, like floorcloths. Clusters of small boys hung in the trees but were shaken down by the police. The streets leading up to the Bulevard Revolucije, where Tito's tribune stood, were barricaded by the police, and in the side-streets the door of every house was guarded by tommy-guns. I was jostled slowly back towards the Teracije. The doors of all the houses were locked, but some people were getting into the new building opposite the Hotel Moskva, and I managed to squeeze in too. I rang a bell on the first floor and a scared old lady opened the door.

'May I come in and watch the parade from above?'

'I'll call the doctor.'

157

A doctor with blue veins at his temples and yellow transparent hands came to me and quaked:

'I don't know whether you can. I don't know whether I dare. I think you'd better ask someone else.'

One flight down and I entered a room hung with photographs of football teams, and there were shelves full of silver cups. Through a window I clambered out on to a rain-shelter projecting from the wall. At least a hundred people were standing on this shelter, including a little girl on a chair, holding a doll. Her father held his rain-coat over her head. Below me the processional route shone in the May-Day rain. Inquisitive people ten deep, and in front of them a line of police.

'But there were more people out last week,' said someone, 'when Kidrić's body was taken to the station on a gun-carriage. That was the first time Jovanka Broz appeared in public, you see.'

Bread and circuses.

First came the machines on wheels, then the machines on foot. First jeeps and Sherman tanks, then troops, who had been waiting since four in the morning to carry out this marching test. They talk scornfully here of the fascist style of marching — but what else was this?

In two hours it was all over. As a finale came the drenched Sports Clubs of Belgrade, the Home Guard, the Ambulance Corps and the Fire Service. Men and women students with shaggy forelocks and carrying dummy rifles brought up the rear. The university curriculum here includes a certain number of weekly drill-hours. Then the police-barriers were broken and in a moment the Maršala Tita became a sea of people.

The room behind the rain-shelter belonged to the *Partizan* Sports Club. Would I like to go out to the *Partizan* Stadium and watch the traditional May-Day match between the *Partizans* and *Crvena Zvezda*?

The *Partizan* Stadium was a cauldron holding 60,000. A motor-road led straight to the grandstand. Hundreds of State-owned and

CD cars were parked outside, and through a big glass door I was taken into one of the diplomats' boxes.

Sports grounds: monuments of a new era, but also instruments of propaganda for dictators. The Colosseum. The Olympia Stadium in Berlin, the Nep Stadium in Budapesth. And here a shallow bowl, where broad running tracks lay between the football ground and the stands, giving a dispersed effect.

The *Partizan* Club is the Yugoslav Army football team, and they win year after year. They toured Sweden in 1950. But they are not the people's favourites; the people say the *Partizans* have everything that other clubs can't get: a huge stadium, troops to build for them, power to commandeer the best players. They have the whole Army behind them, for no one in it is allowed to belong to another club. The *Partizans* are the favourites of the officers, the diplomatic corps, the Party and Tito. But the people's hearts beat for the Red Star, for the Red Star was David versus Goliath.

Applause. Red Stars and *Partizans* on to the ground. After only a minute's play the *Partizans* took the lead by means of shock tactics, and Milovan Djilas, one of the big five on the Central Committee, applauded wildly. Outside the Stadium stood Djilas's sea-green Mercedes sports car. And General Dapčević, the commander-in-chief, smiled.

The Red Stars equalized, but the *Partizans* made it 2–1. Beads of sweat were running down the brow of the portly lady from the Egyptian Legation. For the first minute of the second half the score stood at 3–1 to the *Partizans*; then the Red Stars woke up.

Crvena Zvezda! Crvena Zvezda! Crvena, Crvena! Crvena-a-a!

The *Partizans* took the offensive. The goalkeeper muffed his kick. The ball was poked over the sideline. A *Partizan* beat up an opponent but the referee saw nothing. All round the barrier ran the red letters: The *Partizans* wish you a happy May Day.

A free kick and the Red Stars made it 3–2; a minute later 3–3. A storm of jubilation swept the stands. Umbrellas and coats flew in the air. Someone yelled through a megaphone 'Up the *Partizans!*'

but was forced roughly down on to the bench again. He fought, but was held down like a cat being drowned. A policeman to the rescue, howling at the crowd.

'I'll talk to you afterwards!'

But in the grandstand an icy atmosphere prevailed. The diplomatic corps were pale, the senior officers were pale, and my neighbour crushed his hat in fury.

One seventh of the population of Belgrade was in this stadium, and if ever the mood of the people was to be felt it was here. And I was answered. For ball, numbers on shirts, free kicks, corners, passes and tries and all the rest of it were merely a mask over the real game — the great drama now being played out in the *Partizan* Stadium between State and People. When the State lost the upper hand, the grandstands paled; but what followed was inevitable. As violently as the match had begun, it ended, with an inglorious goal for the *Partizans*.

But the man at my side smoothed out his hat. The wrinkles almost entirely disappeared as he rose contentedly and strode to the exit.

The Mercedes of Milovan Djilas had already gone. It was impossible to get on to a bus or a tram. I walked slowly into the town, and in the Maršala Tita I saw Milovan Djilas in a leather cap, talking to three others: 'Look at me, hobnobbing with the people.'

But ten steps behind him stood three men in very plain clothes. They had their hands in their pockets, and the pockets bulged with something hard.*

Tuesday. Putnik's office stood at the corner of the Maršala Tita and the Bulevard Revolucije, immediately above the Teracije. There I bought a *Führer durch Belgrad*: a *tour de force* of guide-book drivel. I cannot resist quoting these wishful fancies:

'When night falls and thousands of lights shine out, when Bel-

* On January 17, 1954, Djilas was brought low by Party intrigue and deprived of office. The official reason was that he was the author of certain over-liberal articles in *Borba*. The unofficial one was that in other articles Djilas had made insinuations about the wives of high-ranking Communists.

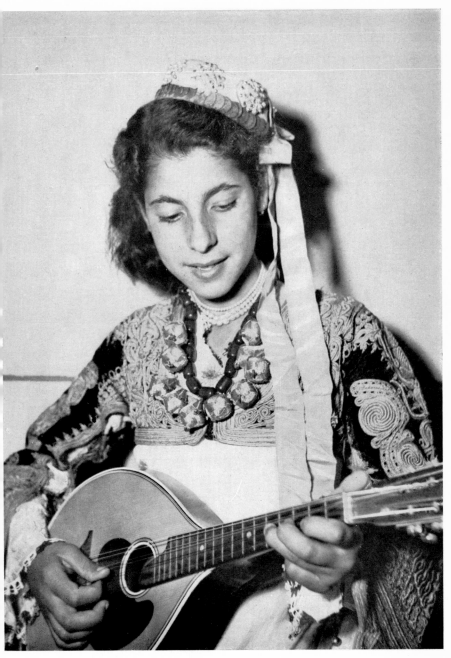

Shquiptar-player from Priština.

Gypsy children in Priština.

grade is radiant in its splendour and cars stream along the streets, the pavements are filled with beautifully dressed people; the people who a few hours ago stood at their machines, sat at their typewriters or draughtsman's tables, bent over school desks or served customers in the shops. From the cafés come the pleasant strains of music, and the streets are emptied as the people enter theatres, cinemas, concert-halls and dance-halls; and next morning, with light hearts, set the pace for the work of their great city.'

Where are the lights? Where is the stream of cars? And the happy people? There are undeniably streets — wide ones. No trams clatter along the Maršala Tita; and that not merely for technical reasons, but also – and perhaps chiefly? – to leave a clear route for military parades.

But if the streets had tongues! Before the war the Maršala Tita was called King Milan's Street, and the present Boulevard of the Revolution, which for a time became the Red Army Boulevard, was King Alexander Street. How many streets changed their names after the war? Half, they say. Marshal Tito has commandeered the two largest, and lesser ones have been shared out among Moše Pijade, Edvard Kardelj, Djilas. . . . Streets cannot protest; they must be a patient mat for every new master. What inglorious mercenaries! Their names lie under them like the burnt cities of Troy. But if they could smile, they would; for stones endure, while names are at the mercy of change and whim. They are never far from silence and oblivion.

Wednesday. The Kalemegda is to Belgrade what Skansen is to Stockholm: a fine green park in which is embedded a fortress, now a museum, of medieval origin. A terrace commands a view over the Sava and its river-steamers. This terrace is the favourite place for *flâneurs*. For there are *flâneurs* in Belgrade, and well-dressed women. How can they afford it? The women here are prettier than any others in Yugoslavia.

The Kneza Mihajla brings one from the Teracije to the Kalemegda. The Kneza Mihajla is one of the main streets in Belgrade, and here was one of my favourite restaurants, the Blue Jadra. The Pariska Ulica runs alongside the Kalemegda, and if one follows it down towards the river, one sees on the left a big, white building in symmetrical, quasi-functional style, and a huge glass porch. This is the French Embassy, amorphous, ponderous and absurd. It's said that in Alexander's day this Embassy was the true seat of government.

The Swedish Legation stands on the opposite side of the road; a grey-brown house, quite unpretentious, but said to be the handsomest legation in Belgrade. Before the war it was owned by a Swiss businessman. Now the Yugoslav State lets it for 12,000 dinars a month (between £15 and £16)!

In a pavilion in the Kalemegda the Art Society has been holding its varnishing day. Only authorized academicians were exhibiting. There was no selection-committee: every member was allowed to show two pictures. Lord, what trash!

In sculpture there were only two names: Rodin and Meštrović. The painters were impressionists. There were a few *fauves*. And the public! With what grim earnestness, with what carefully assumed connoisseur-airs they stood in front of all that rubbish! Yugoslav views on art are those of the beginning of the century. Quite intelligent and in other respects radical-minded people are illiterates in modern art. But Yugoslav painters are a queer race.

They like to introduce themselves as *ak. slikar* — academic painter; and it is significant that *slikar* means photographer as well as painter. All that happened in Paris after 1910 has left these senile tight-rope-walkers of the brush completely unmoved. Picasso? A humbug!

But in Yugoslavia there is little opportunity for modern painting. Here the human spirit is not manifested in isolation but is bound up with material standards and means of production, with cars, farm-machinery and radio-sets. In a place where there is one car to every thousand inhabitants, art must necessarily look like this.

Yet 'isms' have reached Yugoslavia. In Zagreb there is a concrete group led by Murtić. And Lubarda was said to be painting in a style very different from that of his picture in the Culture House of Cetinje.

But to discuss painting in Yugoslavia is very trying to the nerves. Here they have revolutions only to achieve reactionary results.

I was present when modern art came to Dubrovnik. The director of the theatre gave a lecture on 'Modern Art' and ended with Degas and Renoir. At this Ivo Dulčić blew up and protested in Soljka's newspaper: 'There has been some art since then.' Finally a free discussion was announced; it took place in the Culture House of Dubrovnik and was inconclusive: Dulčić was pronounced a bad socialist and the director of the theatre conceded that the term 'modern art' might be stretched to include Cézanne.

I think I shall ring up my friend of Svetji Stefan, Tito's personal architect with the gold cigarette case, Branko Bon. He must have contacts. . . .

Thursday. I went first to the ethnographical museum; it's small but well-arranged. In the evening I saw Branko Bon again; he fetched me from the hotel .

'Now I'll take you to the Authors' Club,' he said; we opened a creaking gate opposite the House of the Yugoslav Army and went down some steps into the basement.

As they say in old novels: judge of my amazement when in this place I met a Swedish lady, Karen Aralica. She had married a Yugoslav painter before the war, and during the war she managed to wangle herself and her son back to Sweden, where she worked at the Free Yugoslav Legation in Stockholm. She was the only member of that staff to return to the Yugoslavia of the new order.

'You'd rather live here than in Sweden?'

'Much rather. This is my country; I feel at home here.'

She had a red feather in her hat – the mere fact of the hat was significant – and wore a well-cut grey suit. She belonged to the upper ten of Belgrade.

'In Sweden everybody works for himself — they're all as insulated as ice-boxes. Here we're all together. There's no snobbery; no one's more important than other people just because he's an artist, good or bad. We're comrades.'

The Aralica family have a telephone. This may be thought an unnecessary observation. But in Belgrade a telephone is a symbol of the upper class.

The Yugoslav Ambassador in Paris sat down at our table; I talked about Spain to a middle-aged man with bright grey eyes behind glasses, not knowing whom I was speaking to; names are always blurred at introductions. But when we had said goodbye Branko Bon asked:

'Well, what do you think of Ivo Andrić?'

I had been sitting and talking nonsense with the greatest writer in Yugoslavia.

Then a man of about thirty-five came and sat on the edge of our table; tall, charming and casual. This was Dapčević, the commander-in-chief. I recognized him from seeing him at the *Partizan* Stadium. He told stories loudly, and the ladies in the room tittered.

Yugoslavia, land of paradox. This house belonged to the Royal Automobile Club. The Croat Authors' Society had annexed a beauty-salon which had once been the meeting-place of the ladies of the Zagreb aristocracy, and the Authors' Society of Montenegro was housed in a confiscated bank. The Swedish Foreign Office had asked Tito to be allowed the use of the house belonging to the Serbian Authors' Society, but Tito refused.

In these latter-day literary salons the atmosphere is spiced with a flavour of rococo. Here may be found literary generals, architects obsessed by wild visions of rebuilding Belgrade as a functionalist dream-city, film producers, ambassadors on leave, theatre-managers. . . . Nor do the ladies of eighteenth century salons lack successors in the Square of the Republic — lovely ladies with long, red-lacquered nails.

What it is to be a writer in Yugoslavia! He gets a minister's pension, he is guaranteed a minimum salary of £15 a month. He is paid 10,000 dinars per 30,000 letters, and for a novel of 400 pages about 300,000. Poets get 50 dinars a line.

I was told this by Alexander Vuco, the secretary of the Authors' Society; silver-haired now, and slightly senile. He was once – long ago – a surrealist.

'Authors don't get royalties,' he said. 'So publishers can't speculate on them. For this results in some writers earning a lot of money, while those who don't sell more than a hundred copies never get the chance to try again. We have no Hemingway, paid at a dollar a word, but neither have we any starving authors working as lift-boys or playing the saw in Variety. In other words, we have not the injustices of the capitalist states. While Andrić earns 50,000 a month, I earn 30,000.'

To think I never asked whether it was not better to be worse paid, to climb the hard way to the stars, to feel a vocation and be prepared to fail — whether all these advantages which gave authors their special standing did not also corrupt them. Whether it was worth anyone's while to be an essayist or short-story writer — to write concisely, economically and clearly. And poets — do they have to chop their lines into shorter lengths to live on them?

But not everyone can win admission to the courts of authorized poetry and a minimum pension of 14,000 dinars. Purgatory came first. I remember a young bard in Zagreb who had published a collection of poems privately, and tried to become a member of the Authors' Society. This meant a public examination in front of a hundred listeners. Miroslav Krleža made a bombastic entry, his puffy cheeks blown out, his hair flopping artistically. The young poet mounted the rostrum with his knees knocking together. The immortal birds of love and death croaked with cracked vocal chords into the hall. The audience blushed with embarrassment. Krleža looked at his shoes. . . .

Sunday. An outbreak of lemonade-bottles in the Kalemegda. Children waving paper flags — Yugoslav and Communist. Trees still wore the green of spring, and sunlight filtered through leaves and branches. The 'Blue Danube' of the loudspeakers drowned the song of the thrushes. But the Danube is a greedy river; below the Kalemegda it drinks up the Sava and flows on eastward, bloated and broad as a lake.

Monday. The Partisan Museum in the Kalemegda. Execution of a Partisan; a photograph, with a German soldier behind the camera. Muscular hands hold the Partisan by hair and body, bending his head forward. The axe has struck once and its blade, wedged into the neck, has half severed it. Tepid blood seeps from the man's mouth. His eyes – not yet extinguished – stare at the ground. In the background an onlooker smiles contentedly at the scene.

Tuesday. Eloise, an American journalist, told me the following story — but then she has a fertile imagination. How else could she have stayed in Europe for five years, having started with ten dollars in her pocket? She told me that this morning there was a man standing in the entrance hall of the Hotel Balkan; a man in a shabby green overcoat, spectacles, badly-cleaned shoes and with his hair slicked down with water. 'He never looked at me,' said Eloise, 'but I remember seeing him on the Dubrovnik boat. He had no luggage then, either — just a briefcase. He was behind me when we docked at Gruž and followed me to the tram-stop. The tram was full and as I had three pieces of luggage I had to wait for the next. He waited too — with his briefcase. Didn't even try to get on. Afterwards he put up at the same hotel as I did.'

I remembered seeing him in Sarajevo, where he had sat behind me in the café of the Hotel Europa. That green overcoat. He had coffee and I had tea; when I went out through the hall, he went in. He had room 113; mine was 112.

'What do you suppose he's doing here?' said Eloise.

'Probably a commercial traveller,' I said.

'But the people at the American Embassy told me they always have someone fifty yards behind shadowing them . . .'

I went to Topčider, a green hill south of Belgrade. Prince Miloš's castle was there and Tito's guards. A Tatra that was falling to pieces with rust came along the road, carrying five or six passengers. Among them was an old man; but his beard was still black. It was Alexander II's eldest brother. Being slightly feeble-minded he had escaped the same fate.

Thursday. Branko Bon's son has won a prize for his paintings at the children's exhibition in New Delhi, and he was interviewed on the radio. Augustinčić, one of Yugoslavia's most eminent sculptors, sent a telegram of congratulation to his 'colleague.' Augustinčić achieved fame by his statue of Tito which stands in Tito's village outside Zagreb.

'My son is a prodigy,' said Branko Bon.

This evening I went to Branko's place to see little Ranko's cup.

I must admit I was disappointed by his work. Any imaginative, creative child would have painted as he did.

To call Miro a naïvist is like calling a lion a housecat; no one paints the unconscious more consciously. But a naïve child can never be a naïvist, for naïvism is a manner: that is to say an order of intellectual creation requiring no expense of energy.

There was a ring at the door, and a man with snow-white hair and a face so gentle as to border on foolishness came in. This was Petar Lubarda the painter. I had thought somehow that he was younger.

'My aim,' said Petar Lubarda, 'is to create great painting.'

'That's the aim of every painter,' I remarked.

'Understand me. I believe in painting that serves architecture. I believe in architecture that serves painting. I want to paint murals — I don't believe in more intimate stuff. Neither the eighteenth-century art of the salons, nor that of the impressionists; no, canvases have no message for our time. We live in a progressive, social age;

we must make our art accessible to the masses. Therefore the intimate canvas has lost its purpose. . . .'

The gramophone stopped. Branko Bon had managed to get some records from Italy. 'Wonderful music,' said a young general who was there; I've forgotten his name.

Afterwards we went on to the club, and there was Karen Aralica as usual, with her husband. But as I was leaving I collided with two men whom I recognized at once as being from Cetinje: the director of the art gallery, Milos Vušković with his fantastic moustache and pouting lips, and the fiery-faced director of the Liberation Museum, Alexander Prijić.

'Ah, my dear sir, my dear sir!' cried the director of the art gallery. 'Where did you get to?'

'I didn't get anywhere,' I answered. 'A minister intervened.'

'You who loved our wonderful *kaimak*—'

'We're on our way,' said Alexander Prijić.

'Yes, we're on our way.'

'On our way to—'

'Well, where?'

'To the Artists' Congress in Macedonia.'

As we went home the directors from Cetinje reeled under the moon.

'Here,' said Milos Vusković, dramatically, as we crossed the Trg Republike, 'here is the square I trod for fifteen years.'

'But,' said Alexander Prijić.

'But in Cetinje—'

'In Cetinje—'

'Life is quieter, more peaceful, in Cetinje.'

Friday. We went to the terrace-restaurant in the Kalemegda. It must have been one or two o'clock when we left, and I took a taxi.

'Good car, this; it still goes,' said the driver, with hardly any accent, and I asked how it was he spoke so well.

'I get plenty of time,' he said. 'I sit in the car all night and by the light of the street-lamp I've learnt German, English and French.'

'But what does your wife say about being left to sleep alone every night?'

He turned:

'I'm not married. How could I marry? I couldn't support a wife and family.'

This morning in a house in Belgrade, a man and his wife and three children were found hanging from the ceiling, dead. A short note was found: 'It is impossible for us to live under the present régime.'

Saturday. The huge painting of the railway-workers in the confiscated bank of Cetinje has given me no peace.

That five-storey block of flats he lived in: there were four or five identical blocks facing the street. Sunbeams danced there, and between the houses were green trees, and stands for beating carpets on, and children playing with scooters, tricycles and balls.

It might have been on the outskirts of some provincial town in Sweden. Standardized love-nests.

But white and coloured washing fluttered from every balcony.

The stairs were dirty and splashed with whitewash. Inside the main door was a board bearing the names of all those living in the building; here was the wakeful eye of the State. I could see his name there, and the date of his birth: 1907.

There was no name on the door, but I knew this must be his flat. Inside, at least a hundred parrots were screeching — I rang the bell five or six times, and the parrots continued screeching. I thought of painters with twenty cats and writers with birdcages hanging in every corner. Finding that the bell didn't work I banged loudly on the door.

'Welcome,' said Petar Lubarda.

First a hall in the good old Swedish manner, where a man was scraping the floor: krrvipp, krrvipp, krrvipp. . . . Then Petar Lubarda's studio. It was large and light with glass walls, and it ran the whole width of the house. On an easel was a canvas measuring six foot by nine, representing a battle: powerful abstract figures, patches cutting into one another, screaming horses, traces of Picasso. Another canvas: two horses fighting against a blazing blue sky; and a third: a few abstract black lines on a red background. The distance from Cetinje was lengthening.

'The Yugoslav State is arranging an exhibition for me in São Paulo.'

'Your work's different now from what it was just after the war.'

'Yes. I believed in socialism then — I believed that art must support socialism.'

'That's why you painted socialistic realism, as in Cetinje?'

Lubarda stroked his grey-white hair.

'If I'd been a Russian and painted in the manner of that picture, I should have been packed off to Siberia at once. But I admit that picture was a mistake. I was moving away from art.'

'Were you forced to paint like that?'

He shook his head.

'I could paint as I chose. I painted like that because I believed in it.'

'But if you had painted then as you do now, wouldn't you have been called decadent? Wouldn't you have been condemned for making concessions to Western bureaucracy and capitalism?'

'They wouldn't have liked my painting, but nothing would have happened to me.'

Then he hit back:

'If you'd ever been in Moscow you'd know what dictatorship in art means. I was there in 1947, and I can guarantee that not a single picture of any merit has been painted since Stalin came to power. The galleries were full of portraits of Stalin; painters worked exclusively for the State and were utter imbeciles. One couldn't argue with them. They were convinced that what they were doing was great art. They even imagined that they were the finest painters in the world. They were incurable. We Yugoslav painters were also striving for a socialistic order of painting, but we had come to very different conclusions. This was taken note of. Ilja Ehrenburg's wife arranged for me to meet a certain P — who showed himself to be an opponent of dictatorship in art. I also met the director of a museum who secretly loved modern painting, but was forced to hang Stalin-portraits in his gallery.

'Even as early as 1947 we Yugoslavs were considered too radical. We had organized an exhibition in Moscow, and they felt we needed a lesson. Just before we left for home we were to receive mementoes, and we gathered at Vox, the cultural society of Moscow. There we were taken into a room where there was a long table and a number of chairs. In front of each chair was a stack of paper and a pencil.

' "Is this a board meeting?" I asked.

' "We're just going to demonstrate some Western art," they said.

They began the lesson by showing some reproductions of Cezanne.

' "In these pictures," we were informed, "one can't tell whether it's morning or evening."

'Then the impressionists were shown us. Almost every one was described as being corrupted by capitalism. The only one that might pass was Van Gogh.

' "Van Gogh made great mistakes but his intentions were good, because he painted peasants." '

'As the very crown of decadent painting we were shown Picasso, since it was assumed that Picasso was unknown to us. Our host burst out laughing and we were all expected to do the same. Finally they brought out a portfolio of surrealist reproductions.

' "There's a painter called Salvador Dali, a Fascist. Here you have some examples of Fascist painting." '

'I protested,' said Lubarda. 'Neither Fascists nor Nazis had ever painted like Dali. On the other hand I tried in veiled terms to make clear to our host that the Soviet painting of the day differed very little from the painting of Hitler Germany. So I was hardly surprised to learn on my return to Yugoslavia that *Pravda* called me a Fascist and a war-criminal.'

But how would Lubarda have painted if he had been born in Russia — if since childhood he had never heard anything but that the Paris school was the work of the devil and that the task of the artist was to produce realistic likenesses of political leaders, of fiery red factory workers, the glare of furnaces and the blue smoke of factory chimneys, glorious battles and the capture of the German colours in Berlin?

Monday. On the way out to Žemun on the other side of the Sava you pass Great Belgrade. But Great Belgrade is nothing but a concrete skeleton; building was started here immediately after the war, in the days of illusion. A House of Parliament and I don't know what else. But the money gave out, and to crown everything the concrete began to settle in the soft ground. They blamed the sandy soil, they blamed the decentralization-plan. These buildings are an expression of the old spirit, and are at variance with the principle of decentralization. It was the same with the new TUC building opposite the offices of *Borba* and the Central Committee; a new palace was begun during the Soviet period, but one day the money-box was empty and the workers left their scaffolding and went home.

Since all the other tables in the pavement café outside the Hotel Balkan were occupied, the little man with rheumatic fingers sat down at mine. He was an office-worker somewhere; we mixed German, English, French and Serbian, and understood each other. I asked, as only a foreigner can ask:
'Are you a Communist?'
He deprecated in a damped-down voice:
'No, no, no!'
'Do you like Tito?'
He pondered, and then said:
'That's a very difficult question.'
'Well, what about the other leaders: Ranković, Djilas, Kardelj, Pijade, Popović?'
He looked at me with scared eyes.

'I'm only a little man — a very little man. But they—! They are so big—'

Later he said:

'If you go to Rome, will you look up my brother? He told my mother one afternoon that he was going to play football and the next we heard of him was a card posted in Italy. I was arrested for that, but it was the truth so I got off with a month.'

Tuesday. Srbo-Čoop rang up to ask if I would like to see a co-operative farm.

Two men were sleeping on the steps. We woke them.

'How do we get to Resnik?' we asked.

One pointed left, the other right. Then they went to sleep again.

We reversed and turned on to a broad road.

'This is the new road to Resnik,' said a woman carrying two buckets on a yoke over her shoulders.

We drove for a mile and a half, and then the car sank to the hub-caps in mud. We abandoned the driver and continued on foot. 'We' consisted of the interpreter, a Yugoslav woman who had lived in the States; the Control Woman, broad and sturdy, hard and vigilant — an Anna Pauker with a face like clods of earth; myself; and an American radio-reporter who had turned up at the Hotel Balkan from Japan. He looked like a Jap, with sharp brown eyes.

We pressed on through the mud between small, fenced-in farm-buildings with their fresh green fruit-trees, their acrid smell of dung and the fierce dogs that thrust their noses through the fence and barked dementedly. A little boy was driving a herd of pigs. Five white cows splashed past, majestic as the sacred cows of India. In the middle of the village and the mire was the *zadruga*.

'We don't claim that this is a model co-operative,' said the Anna Pauker woman. 'On the contrary, production here has been no more than moderate.'

The walls of the grey-painted hall were flaking. Pin-ups: Tito and Lenin. Beside them a darker square, once occupied by Stalin. The members of the co-operative clumped in on heavy, muddy feet. They were old men with white, drooping moustaches and young men with hands as big as spades. They lit their pipes and sat down with their backs against the wall. The pretty English-speaking interpreter sat down at a table and the Anna Pauker woman waited unsmilingly for my questions.

But what was I to ask these men, and what could they reply? Could I ask them about the co-operative system? They would seek their answers in the Anna Pauker woman's eyes. So I asked if anyone knew the name of the capital of Sweden.

The peasants scratched their heads, conferred with one another and agreed at last on Stockholm. They looked embarrassed, but brightened when I told them that they were right, and that few Swedish peasants would know the name of the capital of Yugoslavia.

Then we talked about their co-operative. In Resnik, the peasants told me, there were four hundred farms, of which thirty-eight belonged to the farmworkers' co-operative, the rest being independent. The families of the thirty-eight numbered two hundred individuals, but only one hundred and twenty were employed in the co-operative. Their combined acreage was about 189 hectares (470 acres), that is to say three and a half acres per worker employed.

'Have you ever thought of dissolving your co-operative?'

No, they hadn't; indeed they planned to go in for cattle-breeding on a larger scale next year. At the moment the co-operative had only thirty cows — one to every four producers.

'Are there any organized Communists among you?'

Some looked askance at the Anna Pauker woman, but she neither nodded nor shook her head.

No, no Communists.

'But in the village?'

About thirty-seven.

'How much does a worker earn?'

It varied. It depended on the weather. Last year, which was a bad year, about 4s. 6d. a day, but a year like this one promised better: at least 6s.

A little way outside the village were the stables and silos of the Farmworkers' Co-operative. A few children were sitting on some steps picking their noses. Everything was dead and desolate and it was a Tuesday in May. Outside the cartshed stood an over-grown caterpillar tractor, out of date and eaten up with rust.

'The Italians left this behind, but we have another — a new one.'

Proud hands opened a double door and there it stood: a brand new reaper-binder with shining blades. The Anna Pauker woman spoke for the first time: 'Yugoslav manufacture.'

After that we drank beer in the canteen. Two bearded men in leather caps, tattered overalls and high boots sat at a table playing chess.

'They're training for our chess-championship.'

Express message from the village: our driver and a pair of oxen had after two hours succeeded in extracting the car from the mud. And so we left Resnik.

13. THE IRON GATE

DUSK was falling over Belgrade. At the quay below the Kalemegda lay the white shadow of the river-steamer *Split*, with her paddle-wheels bathing in the water. At the gang-plank waited a packed throng of men and women, in coarse clothes, their bundles on their backs. Others stood quite still as if paralysed, with their baskets set down in front of them. The river was black and mute, and beyond flickered the lamps of Zemun. Above the lights of the city were like fireflies, flaring up and fading. A tall funnel . . . shiny covers to the paddle-wheels . . . people on the quay.

Hours of farewell.

Time of departure, twenty minutes to eight; passengers, seven hundred — a hundred or so more than was allowed — already packed into the boat. Ten minutes later the gang-plank was drawn in, the bell rang and the wheels scooped. Cautiously the white shadow detached itself from the quay.

It was then that a taxi came clattering downhill from the town.

Brakes were jammed on; two men hurled themselves out and elbowed their way through the mob. Policemen dashed up — but the men had thrown their baggage on to the sloping cover of the paddle-wheel and were climbing like monkeys over the railing of the quay; they leaped for the boat — and now she was a couple of yards from shore.

A policeman came down on to the wheel-cover:

'What the devil—'

Too late.

The distance from the landing stage widened to ten, twenty, thirty yards – midstream on the Sava – we were paddling downriver towards Pančevo and the Danube. Belgrade drowned in the night.

The policeman, suspiciously:

'Who the devil —'

Both men fished out passport and identity-card, and permits, valid for three days, to visit the frontier of Yugoslavia and Rumania.

So began my Danube voyage along the Iron Curtain: with a leap over a bit of the Sava.

But who was the other man? Who was Milenko Milović?

I met him in Belgrade, in the street: a young man with a Montenegrin moustache.

'You're from Sweden,' he said.

'And you speak Swedish,' I answered.

But why Milenko speaks Swedish is a long story which I can't tell here. It begins with a pair of red Partisan stockings and ends with a flight over the Norwegian mountains into Sweden.

The bank slunk backwards. That night we paraded our ideologies under the stars, fired our volleys beneath the unseen smoke from the tall funnel, mobilized all our eloquence and churned out propaganda like arch-demagogues.

But some people can neither convert nor be converted.

Milenko's a rogue, I thought. What a rampart of lies he's thrown up! But what if he *can* explain everything, defend everything — what if it *is* impossible to knock holes in his encircling wall of opinions? However smoothly the gear-wheels engage in his abstract thought-machinery, the devil sees his sins. Never mind if he won't yield. Never mind. . . . He's not alone in his incorrigible idiocy.

And that was just what Milenko was thinking — of me. He was thinking that from my point of view I was drawing appropriate if extremely egoistic and on the whole worthless conclusions.

We considered our systematized foolishness with the interest one devotes to a chess-problem, a Latin text or a mathematical formula. A certain intellectual curiosity induced us to try to look into one another and understand one another — but to accept one another's points of view, never! We lacked the emotional qualifications for such a thing.

'You blackguard,' said I to Milenko.

'You blackguard,' said Milenko to me.

'There's this difference,' I said. 'If I thought as you do you wouldn't be able to call me a blackguard.'

'But you see, I don't think as you do,' said Milenko.

For thirty-two hours we travelled along the borders of a closed world — along the very seam of East and West.

It was night now. We still had Yugoslavia on each side of us. Once upon a time this darkness, in which we were sailing to meet the dawn, was a huge, terrifying inland sea, where giant lizards gargled and birds with hairy wings hunted prehistoric fish. To the east the sea was held back by the high plateau now called the Djerdap. But water is stronger than stone, and digs its way through thousands of years of rock to conquer it at last. A vast deluge rolled down towards the Black Sea, draining the inland sea and leaving struggling, gasping fish, floating lizards, the immense plain of Vojvodina, and a river which was one day to be called the Danube, and which on a June night in 1953, was to carry a paddle-steamer of retiring age towards the east.

Her Swedish passenger groped with his feet in the darkness so as not to tread on any outstretched hands, and stumbled down the ladder to the main deck. Where the funnel stretched its neck up from the boiler he could see down into the engine-room. The heat boxed him on the ears. On the extreme edge of this volcano, peasant women lay peacefully sleeping with their children beside them. Old men snored with their backs against the hot funnel. Others slept like cranes, on one leg. A young officer sat on the ladder leading below to the orlop deck and smiled in his sleep, dreaming that a woman came to him. Other men and women lay stretched on pieces of baggage in the gangway between the engine room and the lavatories. They slept as if on featherbeds, transported to a downy unreality, untroubled by those who stepped over their heads on the way to the restaurant, untroubled by the door of the urinal that swung to and fro, wafting waves of suffocating stench through the heat.

A strange, fire-written beauty shone over all these sleeping Serbs. A poem vibrated above them:

> But we who can no longer sleep like cattle
>   standing in our stalls in the shame of our own droppings;
> We who do not sleep on nails —
> have we deserved better than to awake to our mechanized agony?
> Beauty's only cosmetic is dirt. . . .

I was roused by Milenko shaking my head, and when I protested he said:

'No, no — you *must* get up!'

'But it's only six o'clock,' I mumbled.

Daylight was splashing through the scuttle.

'You must see the Iron Curtain. You must see Rumania,' Milenko insisted, and would not be gainsaid.

I put my head out. The Danube was not the Danube of the waltzes, but yellow and vile; not overlaid with dull gold like the Arno, but suppurating with grey-green-yellow slime. We sped through the Djerdap, while wooded hills rushed by us; I could almost have spat on them. This was Rumania.

'Mind they don't shoot your head off!' cried Milenko. 'Look at that watch-tower. The Rumanians have a habit of practising their sniping on the river-steamers.'

On the shore, its feet almost in the water, stood a watch-tower where two grey-clad Rumanian soldiers were on guard. One raised his binoculars and fixed my image on the lens.

'My head's precious,' I said, and withdrew it hastily. Milenko laughed.

'The whole of that shore's stiff with towers. You'd better stay in bed all day.'

Thereupon we cleaned our teeth, dressed and went on deck. So began our voyage along the seam of East and West.

The passage through the Djerdap is sixty miles long. At Belgrade the river had been a mile and a half across; now it narrowed and deepened, shrinking in places to a few hundred yards. Sometimes the current drove us over to the Rumanian side, at others close along the Yugoslav bank. We were scraping between two continents.

For thousands of years, Milenko told me, the Iron Gate has been the entrance and exit between East and West. The Roman Emperors passed through the Djerdap. In the first century Tiberius built a road along the south side of the Danube, and Trajan reinforced it to pierce through the Iron Gate.

This is one of the fiercest, most dangerous reaches in the eastward passage. Where the Djerdap ends, one is met by a landscape of a very different nature: a plain as soft as a cushion. But the river — the river is swift and virile and full of dangerous currents, so that boats must by-pass this stretch through a little canal at Sip.

Going downstream it's not difficult to get through the canal, said Milenko, but against the current, for small craft especially, it can be a struggle; so there is a locomotive to tow them. Like the Danube, the Sip canal is international water, but the engine is Yugoslav, and a Russian skipper cannot so degrade himself as to be pulled along by a miserable little Yugoslav locomotive. Up to quite a short time ago the shipping from Soviet Russia and the satellite states had orders to struggle through unaided. Then the vessels used to get stuck, and block the canal so that other boats could pass neither up nor down. But they're to bring this question up at an international court, said Milenko.

The *Split* glided through the canal and out on to the waters of the plain. By the canal the engine blinked knowingly and the engine-driver stood beside it in a sooty singlet, drinking beer. But the Iron Gate was conquered. Upstream towards the Djerdap panted Hungarian, Czech and Rumanian strings of barges, flying a faded hammer-and-sickle flag. At these moments, at these encounters, a belt of cold fell over the spring warmth of the Danube. No smiles were exchanged, only a chilly curiosity. Only frosty thoughts: those are the deserters! Those are the ones who betrayed our cause!

Two towns floated up ahead, Turnu-Severin on the Rumanian side, and opposite, Kladovo. Turnu-Severin had grown up round the castle of Emperor Alexander Severus and the bridge of the Emperor Trajan. Of this only the abutments remained. And Turnu-Severin was a town that kept its mouth shut, close-lipped and morose. It was Sunday, hence perhaps the silence. The welding-plant at the docks had closed its lips over its heat-rays. A coloured portrait of Stalin, looking like a clipping from a comic paper, caught the eye on the gable-end of a factory.

'See that warehouse?' said a sailor. 'I worked there before 1948; only just managed to get back . . .'

After a few minutes' silence:

'And do you see that village?' (Turnu-Severin was already behind us.) 'Do you see all those empty houses? The people who lived in them have been evacuated inland.'

I saw villages and a few sheep. A few people, a number of soldiers, and many watch-towers.

The sailor talked of Rumanian women, the mate talked of Rumanian nights and the captain talked of three Rumanian women who had fled a few weeks before. When they saw the *Split* approaching they jumped into the water and tried to swim after her to Yugoslavia. But they were caught in one of the searchlights from the watchtower; shots echoed across the water and they sank, one after the other.

'But that's all too common,' said the captain. 'The only unusual thing about it was that they were women. . . .'

I saw the Rumanian shore, but I saw it behind six foot of barbed wire — I saw forts and pillboxes and parapets. On the Yugoslav side I saw women in yellow skirts and black aprons strewn with silken roses, and men in national dress; it was Sunday.

Soil and meadows have no political programme, villages do not distribute propaganda; mountains — as Orjen had once been for me in Dubrovnik — may become a symbol of freedom, but they can never be freedom itself. As I lay stripped to the waist in the sun on one of the benches of the upper deck – the air was quivering like a street of blue asphalt – I was ready to maintain that matter cannot only symbolize a psychic or spiritual condition, but that in certain circumstances it could *be* that condition. As with half-closed eyes I watched the green meadows dancing by, the cows bathing in the river, an ox-cart being whipped along, its wheels almost submerged in the water; fishermen in hollowed tree-trunks and with the same round, glittering seine as is used by the fishermen of Stockholm – when I saw the alders, poplars and walnut-trees, and the slopes foaming green with vines – I felt that living cells and dead matter were all shot through with light and life and freedom.

Turning my head I saw Rumania; I saw the desolation of the shore, the trees' loneliness. No women scrubbed their linen in the yellow Danube water. No oxen plunged their cloven hooves into the mud. I saw watch-towers and barbed wire: a front line, strongly supported in the rear by massive redoubts, partly camouflaged, but so badly as rather to emphasize their purpose than to conceal it — their dual purpose of frightening the Yugoslavs and barring the Rumanians' road to freedom; the freedom of Tito's Yugoslavia.

I wondered whether the men in the tower could sense the force radiating from the earth on the Yugoslav side of the Danube, or whether they believed that we – I and the Yugoslavs – were enemies, provocateurs, who had betrayed land and people to the capitalists, the Vatican and the Western imperialists. Whether they imagined that at any moment we might thrust our landing-craft over the river to snatch factories from the workers, fields from the peasants.

Did they really believe all that? Were they, too, the helpless victims of the propaganda machine? If not, why did the men with the binoculars stay where they were? Why didn't they swim across the river?

Worlds and myths jostled one another, and the loudspeaker on the deck bawled the news from Belgrade. But after the news came dance-music, and Yugoslav schoolgirls of fifteen – girls with long plaits – danced on the after-deck.

Why did we meet no boats carrying dancing Rumanian children?

And while the steamer crept nearer to the point where the frontiers of Yugoslavia, Rumania and Bulgaria meet, something happened to relieve the sense of physical tension between two worlds. And what happened was the dancing schoolgirls. One of them was sent to me as ambassador, and she asked me blushing:

'Do you speak English?'

And then shyly.

'Will you tell us about your country?'

Milenko had been telling tales out of school.

But they made a ring round me, from which there was no escape.

I asked them how it was they spoke English so well.

'We don't speak it well; we have only been learning it for two years at school. We can talk Russian too. We learned Russian some years ago, before we were allowed to start English. We come from Niš. It's the end of term and we're on a school outing. Do you know where Niš is? A very beautiful town — our town. . . .'

I told them about the midnight sun, and Lapps and reindeer, about the snow, about nights in Norrland which are like days; about Stockholm and the King and all the cars there are — about everything I thought might interest them because it differed from things in their own world. It's no easy matter to speak about one's country, especially to twenty Yugoslav schoolgirls. I suppose I talked for ten minutes. Tree and villages swept past, and when I ended one of the girls said:

'And Yugoslavia — isn't Yugoslavia a beautiful country?'

I told them that no country is more beautiful than another, but that for me Yugoslavia was one of the most beautiful. Their eyes were begging for that answer, but I could give it sincerely. They smiled and said.

'We're proud of living in Yugoslavia. We're glad to live in such a lovely country.'

They were, as girls are everywhere, happy and unhappy in the present and looking forward to the future. One wanted to be a school-teacher, another a doctor, a third a librarian. One said, 'I hope I shall get married.' But one girl, fragile as a wild poppy, with the sort of eyes that make high-school boys write high-school poetry and stand in doorways opposite the beloved's house, just to see her come out, asked me gravely:

'Who's your favourite actor?'

Hoping to hit on the right one I said:

'Humphrey Bogart.'

'Oh!' she said. 'Don't you like Laurence Olivier?'

'Goodness, how stupid of me,' I said. 'How could I forget him? I think I like him best of all.'

'How extraordinary,' she whispered breathlessly. 'So do I!'

'Do you want to go on the stage?' I asked.

'How did you guess?' Her lips were quivering.

Perhaps I ought to have talked to them about the difference between Swedish schoolgirls and Yugoslav ones, instead of about snow and the northern lights. I ought to have said:

'I'll talk about poetry.'

Poetry is a sublime myth. This is not to be taken as a general observation, but as a personal and moreover extremely ephemeral one, born of the moment and of the shores gliding away behind us. And how many shores did I not fleetingly touch on this journey: those of the Dalmatian islands, of Boka Kotorska, of Montenegro, and now:

There is a world where poetry is reality, but that world is no longer ours. For only if we will believe in the untruth: that love is an invisible, spiritual essence of the best that is in existence, and that love takes possession of us to bring us nearer to the primal image of all things — only if we have this foolish conception have we made poetry our refuge.

Skoplje, the most Oriental town in Yugoslavia.

Macedonian blacksmiths.

May sunshine on the Turkish gardens of Skoplje.

The direct descendant of the victor of Kossovo, in 1389, now guards his ancestor's tomb. (*Below*) Priština's new theatre.

I don't mean to despise the man of sense and praise the fool, but
– and especially then, as the sky sailed past untouched and pure –
I was persuaded that the man who has never during part of his life,
or as part of his life's pattern, been unaware, and sought to defend
his unawareness with poetry – the man, in other words, who has
never dwelt in the world of poetic myth – has endured a degrading
poverty.

But how shall she whom we have fed with our Kinsey reports,
our sexual instruction, our dailies and weeklies which increase their
circulation in the sacred name of factual enlightenment — how shall
she whom we have helped to strip love of every gleam of poetry,
need poetry? By this I don't mean the reading or writing of
poems, but poetic living; the transmutation of the world into a
poem, life into a garden or any other kind of lyrical landscape, such
as the one we were just passing through. To live out one's day, to
express one's moods, in poetry; in that sense there are very few
modern girls – very few Swedish girls – who are poetic. They have
lost the subtler links with existence; they have lost the power to live
musically.

I don't know, but I believe – at any rate I believed then as my
eyes travelled up the tall funnel of the *Split* and sailed back with the
smoke – that such poetic living is closely bound up with humility
in one's attitude to life. At any rate that should be so. . . .

The women who lay sleeping above the furnaces. . . . In all their
ugliness, the drama and the humility of their sleep turned them into
poetry.

And these twenty schoolgirls from Niš, dancing on the deck. . . .

My thoughts were interrupted by a box on the ear from the fog-
horn. A bump followed, and general tumult among the passengers.
We had come alongside the landing-stage of Prahovo.

Prahovo is a community of a few hundred people. Six or seven
miles further on, the Danube makes a feint to the right and from
being the boundary between Yugoslavia and Rumania it becomes
that between Rumania and Bulgaria. A black locomotive stood

blowing its nose in front of its sooty coaches; this was the train for Niš which was to leave in a few hours, and which meanwhile kept company with the white steamer puffing at the pontoon-landing stage.

Light clouds scudded before the wind on transparent sails, playing with their shadows on the water and on the railway-station, and on villagers in their Sunday clothes. The vineyards were terraced above the river, and the grassy slopes quivered with vermilion poppies. *Ergo*, a landscape that was peaceful and carefree. One could lie and look up at the cloud dragons jostling and devouring one another. One could feel the tiny needle-points of grass in one's back. Meanwhile train and boat chatted together, exchanging gossip from Belgrade and Niš. The girls picked poppies. There came the soughing wing-beats of four wild duck; they sank down over the river, rose again and vanished into Rumania. Sunday. A Sunday in June.

As the train gave a warning hoot some of the girls came running up with bunches of poppies.

'Take these! A souvenir of the girls from Niš!'

The train puffed off. The *Split* drew away from the landing-stage. Return journey. Upstream.

Dusk fell. The shores were quenched in the second night of the journey. The river: first mauve as hyacinths, then black as the sky. From time to time a searchlight tickled the surface of the water with its cone of brightness.

When we woke next morning the boat had begun to pound up the river. The land to the north of us was still Rumania.

It was like seeing a film backwards. Our smoke billowed over Lassovo at the entrance to the Djerdap. The wooded hills lifted their bodies on each side of us. At our eight or ten knots and with our boiler crimson with wrath, we managed to overtake a Czech tug-boat towing sixteen barges in pairs.

Later, in the afternoon, as I was drinking *slivovica* with the three ship's policemen, we left the Djerdap. The sun was now behind Gobolac, the best preserved of all the medieval fortresses in Serbia, once the first and strongest bolt on the Iron Gate.

Towards evening, Smederovo. Rumania lay behind us. Round Smederovo runs the strongest girdle-wall in Serbia: a chain of massive ruined towers, partly blown up by the Germans one autumn day in 1941.

At about ten o'clock (only an hour late by the time-table) Belgrade kindled its lights before us. A shadow rose over the water: the bridge over the Sava. The Danube had left us.

Then we heard shouts of 'Stop! Stop!'

The funnel, which must be lowered to pass under the bridge, had jammed. Full speed astern — the paddlewheels braked convulsively and then began turning backwards; but still the span of the bridge bore down upon us. The engine fell silent, and what it failed to do the current accomplished: it seized the vessel and slowly carried us back towards the Danube. The lights of the city shrank, the shadow of the bridge faded and was swallowed up in night.

Was the Iron Gate summoning up all its pagan strength to force us back into its gullet?

Then with a rattle the funnel sank through the deck; the hull shuddered and the paddles scooped. The Iron Gate had lost its prey. Almost noiselessly we glided under the bridge and made fast below the Kalemegda.

My bunch of meadow-flowers had faded, but I couldn't see that. At night all flowers are black.

14. ARRIVAL IN THE BALKANS

IN the fifth month of my stay in Yugoslavia I arrived one morning in the Balkans.

The journey to Priština was not my idea, but that of Djordje Karaklajić, the head of the folk-music department at Radio Belgrade. It was in Priština that the first musical festival of the autonomous Albanian People's Republic of Kossovo and Metohia was to be held.

'I warn you,' said Karaklajić, 'it's not Paradise you're going to, but the most primitive region in all Yugoslavia.'

And off we went.

Yugoslav long-distance trains travel at night. When morning hammered on the windows I was 280 miles south of Belgrade. I changed to Kossovopolje; my old train went on to Skoplje. In the new one sat dirty, scratching women in baggy Turkish trousers. A blind singer – a boy of eighteen – stumbled from compartment to compartment, led by a child of six. He sang harshly in a falsetto voice, but his song had a strange rhythm like that of the train-wheels and his hands danced on a *darbuka*.

'When we gypsies were in Germany,' he sang. 'When we gypsies were in Germany, they mutilated our bodies and burned our eyes. When we gypsies were in Belsen and Buchenwald and Dachau. . . . And all from our village were there, our Macedonian gypsy village. When we gypsies were in Germany, when we—'

I made my entry into the Balkans in a lurching, squeaking cab drawn by two horses. And of those days in Macedonia and in the Albanian country of the *shquiptar*-players I will speak briefly, for now my farewell to Yugoslavia is drawing near.

In Priština there was a newly-built town hall of red brick, and a new, soiled theatre surmounted by the Communist star. Outside this there was a pandemonium of bleating sheep. The Priština Radio Station broadcast in Turkish, Albanian, Macedonian and Serbian, for all these four languages are spoken in Kossovo. Craftsmen's booths yawned on to the street: the wheelwright, the farrier and the shoemaker with his sour leather.

Yet another new world, where a masterless cow lay snoozing on the steps of the theatre and my cart slid over something soft. A squeal cut through the stench of leather and dried carcasses swarming with rabid flies, and a dog with blood dripping from its severed leg limped howling down the little open drain that ran through the town.

This was Priština, with its theatre and stadium and who knows what else; Priština, a capital without sewers, piped water or paved streets.

The hotel I stayed at was called the Hotel Nova Jugoslavija. There I met Karaklajić, also a radio technician, a reporter from the newspaper *Borba*, and a photographer sent out by an official photographic bureau in Belgrade. We were all packed into one room and shared one towel, one wash-basin and jug, a 15-watt ceiling bulb and a privy which I cannot describe; the whole hotel reeked of stale urine. Everyone regarded the trip to Priština as more or less of a punishment.

'Good God!' cried Karaklajić. 'I've forgotten my DDT!'

'All's well,' said the photographer soothingly. 'I've brought two tins of it.'

I stayed in Priština for three days. On the second, the Belgrade contingent left and that night I shared the room with a Greek from Salonika and three peasants, but which the Greek was I never discovered, since they were all equally bearded and filthy. To photograph dirty people is one thing — but to sleep with them —! One rose at four in the morning, the second at five, the third at six; and by the time the fourth got up at seven the air in the room was denser than glue. All slept with their clothes on and none of them used the wash-basin.

From Priština I went to Kossovo, the Waterloo of the South Slavs.

An hour's journey through meadows of red, poppy-like flowers which are to be found here and nowhere else; on the western horizon the white range called Šar Planina, beyond which lay Albania. The driver of the cart cried 'Ptr-o-o' and reined in beside a Turkish tomb covered by a dome and ringed by a wall. The whole stood on a hillock with a view over a golden plain of gentle hollows. Those who have power to see the spirits of the past would behold here, by night, the flash of sabres in the moonlight; they would hear death-rattles and the pounding of thousands of hooves, and smell the acrid smell of blood.

For this is Kossovo.

It was here, on 15th June, 1389, after four days' fighting, that the Turks won their decisive victory, and dominion over most of the Balkans for the next five hundred years. Four days which made of the Balkans a bridgehead into Europe for minarets, veiled women and sweet Turkish coffee. The year 1389 and Kossovo form a climax to Turkish expansion in the northwest, just as 1571 and Lepanto were the turning-point, and the loss of Sarajevo in 1878 and the Balkan war of 1912 the departure.

A round-shouldered Turk turned the key of the tomb and then said:

'Do you know Tito?'

Without waiting for my answer he went on:

'The world is full of infamy. Here lies the great Sultan Hudavendigar Murat who conquered at Kossovo – here lies the great Murat, Ohrau's son, who died at Kossovo; and here lies the great Murat who was murdered by the traitor Miloš Obilić. Miloš came here to beg mercy for the Slavs, and then drew his sword and ripped up Murat's stomach. Now Miloš is celebrated as the great national hero – but, ah! the great Murat was a greater man, and I am his descendant.

'Who would dare to leave the dust of a man like Murat to the hands of outsiders — perhaps even Christians? Therefore Murat's family came to Europe to guard great Murat's tomb. We who claim great Murat for our ancestor have lived here for five hundred years. The other tombs you see outside are those of Murat's son and grandson, of my father, my grandfather and my great-grandfather; for the great Murat has destined us to die in this place. Look at this document,' said the Turk. 'It was drawn up by Alexander II and declares that we of the blood of Murat are the rightful guardians of his tomb, and all sultans and kings through all the ages have set their hands to similar documents.

'But the world is full of infamy,' said the Turk. 'One day a man came here and told me the tomb had been nationalized and was now under State guardianship; and another man calling himself an expert came along waving stamped papers and saying he was the official curator of Murat's tomb. But by Allah, how can anyone be expert at guarding Murat's tomb except Murat's descendants to the sixteenth or twentieth generation?

'I have written several letters to Belgrade about this,' said the Turk. 'I have had no answer. But I am sure that you can put my case to Tito when you get back to Belgrade. For the great Murat cannot endure that a man smelling of Christian blood should take tips for showing his remains.'

I promised that if I met Tito I would convey the Turk's views, but when I did get back to Belgrade it was too late. An invitation to Tito's birthday-party lay amongst the mail awaiting me, but while Tito was celebrating the completion of his sixty-first year I was still in Priština. And from Priština I made another expedition, this time to the medieval Greek Orthodox monastery at Gračanica. The church kept watch over the plain like a yellow and black striped spider, with the great warts of its cupolas on its back. Here was Kafka's cockroach petrified and anchored to the Balkans. But to Vivin or Bombois or any other naïvist, Gračanica would have been an experience of wonderful aesthetic purity.

The empty court round this monster was enclosed on three sides by a wall of low houses and loggias, and at the back of the church was the monastery itself. On one of the loggias a woman was hanging out her newly-washed wool to dry. Gigantic vapour-mushrooms thrust into the sky, to turn grey and explode; rain, soft and dry as pollen, fell on Gračanica.

But the church was full of dark, smoke-blackened frescoes. In Macedonia there are perhaps fifty monasteries with similar medieval murals, which the Yugoslavs claim are Giottos before Giotto, Cimabues before Cimabue. But the monastery of Gračanica is perhaps the mightiest. It was there that St John's eyes were put out with the points of Turkish sabres.

I stayed in Priština for three days.

Villagers from Rugovo had come down from the mountains in their white, close-fitting costumes and they danced the woman-dance, in which two men dance against each other with swords until one or other falls down exhausted. To the sound of the ecstatic *surla* there awoke in me a longing for another journey: a longing to follow the road from Titograd along the Albanian border through Rugovo to Peć. But this journey through Yugoslavia's most barbarous region must be postponed to some other time, for now the summer was starting to blaze down over Macedonia and my final departure was near.

In the square in front of the Orthodox Church in Priština stood the terrible beggars of Priština, with faces like soft slime; and there stood the bridal pair — that fantastic pair: the bride in a veil that was a curtain and the bridegroom in a black suit and brand new handball-shoes.

In the gypsy town the blind boy sang his song about the gypsies' sufferings in Germany, while at the sports ground the mayor sat watching the finale of the great festival, in which all the girls were doing gymnastics and forming letters: *Živio Tito*.

At dawn I took leave of Priština and the *shquiptar*-players, and went on to Skoplje, the capital of Macedonia; and of this place too, with its mosques and villas and gardens, much might be told and most escaped my eyes. For not until my sixth month in Yugoslavia did I grasp the fact that I had reached the Balkans.

But it was too late.

I returned to Belgrade.

On my last evening in Belgrade I went to the Kalemegda. On the slopes below there is an Orthodox church. I knew it was left open at night and so I went in. I stood in there perfectly still, filled with the darkness. Then I struck a match and for a short second there came the glint of dim icons and brass. Then I came out.

Two shadows sprang out of the bushes; they were Rankovic's police.

'We arrest you in the name of the law.'

PART III

15. IN RETROSPECT

HOW Yugoslavia inspired me! Long after I left it, it began working in me again, and during the writing of this book I've been filled at times with such exaltation that I was unable to sit still at the typewriter; I had to get up and walk back and forth, back and forth in my little room – my cell in this block of flats – this prison – where I've been writing. But as I was marching up and down like this the walls fell away and the roof opened and vanished, with all its homes and worlds and radio-sets above my head – Pettersson's and Bergström's and Andersson's, and some new arrival's whose cooking-smells haven't had time to leak out on to the stairs. The sky was above me: not our smug Swedish sky, but the burning blue of Dalmatia or the pale green of Smederovo. And round me rose the crags of Montenegro, as if to protect me, and the Atlantic plain that is Vojvodina.

Can anything that is thoroughly bad liberate one so completely from the ordered chill of our cushioned existence, and penetrate everything with its rays?

But perhaps I couldn't have attained to that healing Yugoslav warmth if I hadn't had those gramophone records from Radio Belgrade. How can I ever properly thank Comrade Karaklajić, that infinitely Communistic naïvist, and Dr. Cvjeyko Rihtman of Sarajevo, for initiating me into the secrets of Yugoslav folk-music? This music has drawn me to itself with the power of the not-understood.

How easy to dismiss it as primitive, slightly barbaric, because it lies beyond the barrier where our hearing usually stops, as a child stops at the garden fence, scared of the unknown outside. But those who venture into that unknown. . . .

197

I can understand the cranks who devote their lives to this music. In rapturous tones they tell of their struggles to coax the secret from every melody, and resolve the almost magical complex which is a song from Macedonia, Serbia or Bosnia. Long before the moderns, these people discovered the twelve-note scale, which opened the way to the most subtle nuances and at the same time to startling harmonies. Above all the rhythm, which seldom sticks to a perpetual 3/4 or 4/4 time; not even to 3/5 or 4/7, but loves to stray into the most complicated and elusive play of rhythms in 7/12, and perhaps – why not? – 13/12 or 15/13. Can music more nearly resemble a rolling sea?

And these songs are rendered with such precision, accuracy and purity, that the complexity of them is forgotten – dispelled – in the limpid simplicity of great art.

But first must come much patient work. First the recording, then the solving of the riddle of structure – and that riddle can guard its secret as jealously as an oyster its pearl, for months. But at last revelation will come; then comes the notation, and with that the sublime experience.

The most wonderful thing is that many of the guardians of this treasure, the folk-singers and instrumentalists, can't read a note of music and some not even their own names. Yet they have the capacity to combine the simple with the difficult; they are springs, fountains which sing spontaneously, without desire, without study or analysis.

It was at Hvar that I heard this music first. I don't mean the quartet that sang serenades below my balcony. Their song had indeed great beauty, but it was a sentimental borrowing from the moon, and the moon can never be relied on. No, I was sitting by the radio in the Hotel Dalmacija – it was just before the power station closed down for the night – when a song from Sarajevo, a plaintive *cevdalinka*, suddenly poured forth and penetrated every atom of the room. It was then I decided to go to Sarajevo.

If this country could for me transmute itself into music, why might it not free itself by music? Its essence is imprisoned in the notes and is released with them. It was thanks to my Serbian folk-songs and those from Skoplje that I have been able to finish this book. The sapphire needle in its groove struck fire from my Yugoslavia. But when the sound-arm swung back to sleep, my visions faded.

My journey through Yugoslavia was a journey through poverty, but never have I encountered a poverty more patiently borne.

I saw poverty in Germany after the war, but that was of a different kind. It had come unexpectedly out of the sky, with the bombs. It was visited upon the unworthy and never had time to become a custom, only a fleeting experience. I remember the cave-dwellers of Hamburg who, obstinate and querulous, cleared the ruins of old tins and laid the foundations of industrial revival.

I remember the clochards of Paris who gathered at dawn at Les Cloches opposite Notre Dame. But are they worth our admiration, our respect or our sympathy? Did they not make their choice freely, and is not the stone bed beneath the arch of the bridge consistent with their attitude to life?

But these – the poor of the Bosnian villages, covered with lice and syphilis sores – for such as these poverty was no parenthesis in time, but a permanent state; not a craving but a necessity. But to bear their degradation, they invoked the devil with the most savage oaths ever pronounced in Europe.

Poverty can give strength. Poverty, like war, can rally a nation. It never rallied Spain, where every individual is a whining wretch under the moon. But it united Sweden, croft by croft, cabin by cabin, just as prosperity is now slackening that invisible bond. Penury has whipped the Yugoslavs together and made of them – all internal religious and political rifts notwithstanding – the most virile nation in Europe.

And now I will tell of my return to Sweden. For I reached home at last. After forty-eight hours in the train from Belgrade, the Swedish coastline was once more caught on my retina.

I came home a stranger. The forest of aerials on the roofs was like a radar scanner on the look-out for enemies: keep your distance! For the first few weeks I was obsessed by the feeling that troubles every foreigner in Sweden: that of being shut out. People were all living in their closed worlds, within closed wood-fibre doors, with their marvellous vacuum-cleaners, their new cars gleaming in the street and their weeklies on their knees, while the wireless played Povel Ramel or Alice Babs. I caught sight of a crumpled, yellowing poster: 'Ingrid Bergman weeps outside Norrköping.' Sweden had been shaken to its foundations. But I was a foreigner in my own country.

I got used to it. I got used to it and returned to the point from which I had started my journey. Then I broke down the walls and life flowed by in constant preoccupation with trifles, leaving no trace, carving no wrinkles. Why shouldn't I adapt myself? Had I the right to be a revolutionary? Had I the right to think for myself when licence-holders sacrificed millions so that the radio might think for me, and when the kings of press and film devoted their capital to sparing me the trouble of using my brain? Had I the right to doubt the wisdom of the hurried introduction of television into Sweden, when television can unburden our people from the last vestiges of independent thinking?

At any rate I bought a 1930 Ford tourer and settled down in a fishing-village somewhere on the west coast. I was near the sea, and gulls cut the barely discernible line between sea and sky. I used to sit on a little hill, where the grass pushed needles through my trouser-legs and butterflies rested on my skin. Off to the island chuffed the fishing-boat crammed with tourists, and by the jetty rocked the red mahogany cabin-cruiser of the margarine tycoon. Summer visitors sat on their fretwork verandahs reading letters from town. The days were enveloped in luke-warm peace and the nights in the peace of pale stars. And beyond all this the blue-green ridge of the hills.

The road up to the main highway was bordered by yellow and green fields: a replete landscape chewing the cud of itself methodically and incessantly. In the light of dawn the fields bathed in phosphorescent milk, the crickets played, and somewhere someone was lighting a pipe and switching on the wireless; there had been only a second between dusk and day.

All was so serene, that even when later on the thunderclouds rode up, they shed their lightnings chiefly for the sake of decoration.

I had my house and my old car right down by the sea. Only a narrow strip of shingle separated me from the water. Here I would be seized at times by a metaphysical claustrophobia: the fear of living on the inside of a space that repelled all wonder and returned answers like an echo of the questions. The waves and the rattle of pebbles, like prisoners' chains, were the only movement in a petrified world. With this sensuous evidence of our limitations the need of a speedy release became explosive. I jumped into my car and, prepared for any blood-sacrifice, I danced along the roads until the grip on me, the claws in my heart, relaxed.

When the summer visitors had gone, when all the lacquered girls had returned to their towns, I left myself behind. It was then that the return to Yugoslavia – Yugoslavia not as a geographic but as a spiritual concept – began.

One day I received a letter postmarked Niš, Yugoslavia, and I should like you to read it, since it gives so much of the Yugoslav national character and bears out one of the chapters I planned when I was there, while impressions were still fresh. Remember that the girl writing to me is sixteen years old. Unfortunately I don't know which of the girls she was, on that Danube voyage through the Djerdap.

Dear Mr. S.

I wonder how to begin a letter to a man I have met once in my life, a man who is also a stranger and probably knows very little about the soul of our people. I ask myself what you will think and how you will interpret my words. But we Yugoslavs are a very sincere and frank people, and I hope you will understand me in that way. When we met and talked on our journey through the Djerdap it was a very interesting experience for me. I was very excited when I told them about it at home, but my mother doubted my knowledge of English. It was the first time I tried to talk English to a foreigner and what was most important, to someone who wrote articles and perhaps books.

I read much and know many classical books. Perhaps I don't know their full meaning but I feel when a book is good. And when you said you were going to write about Yugoslavia I was proud. And I dreamed that some pages in your book would be about your meeting with the Yugoslav girls from the high school in Niš.

Yours sincerely,
Olga Kontić.

What girl in Sweden or America would be proud that a foreigner should visit her country in order to write about it? Or talk so gravely about 'the soul of our people?' What sixteen-year-old believes in souls? What sixteen-year-old doesn't know all about everything already, and hasn't sold her illusions cheap?

It was because Olga Kontić was no exception that I felt at home in her country. It was because there were few like her here that I felt a stranger in Sweden.

My freedom was greater in Yugoslavia. And the people's freedom was greater.

Free in Yugoslavia! Free in a Communist country: a police-state where a couple of days before my departure I had been arrested as I came out of a church, because Church competes with State for the human soul.

The purely external advantages of freedom are perhaps not so very important. What good do all our political parties do us, our freedom to vote for any party we like, our freedom to say what we like when we don't achieve freedom within ourselves; when we let others do our thinking for us and order our lives in accordance with mass-distributed rubber stamps?

I will now proclaim a paradox which will make you jump: there is freedom in Yugoslavia, because Yugoslavs are spiritually independent. They bear the mark of independence on their foreheads: simplicity, humility, self-sufficiency, genuineness. Such people have something to sacrifice for others, something they dare give others.

This is why I want Yugoslavia to be left in peace. I don't believe it needs either our perfect telephone system or our magical baking-powder.

But I also realize that it's useless to fight these things, and that Yugoslavia too must accept them — Mickey Mouse and comics and all the rest; and that Olga Kontić and those with hearts like hers will be a lost generation.

Unfortunately Communism too is striving for the same goal, and no policy exists which does not include Mickey Mouse in its pro-gramme. Since there is no alternative – since the bait offered by all parties is the promise of a higher material standard of living (it's only the difference in method that divides them) – I prefer to stand outside. So long as no party exists with other aims than those of material advantage, I care as little to be a Communist as to be a democrat or a conservative.

Do you remember how often I talked about myths — the Yugoslav myths, as I called them? I promised to revert to the subject one day, and I shall do that now, since it's bound up with what I've just written.

I can see nothing for it but to live on myths. Life otherwise would be unendurable.

Are we then to condemn a régime which fosters the national myth, transparent though it may be to us? Is it not somehow moving and right that a young nation should encourage faith in heroes and partisans? A nation's heroes always belong to the period of its youth, when it gave its blood for its independence. Such hero-myths are of course partly the work of the State — a propaganda-trick, some might call it. (We used to marvel at Tito's ability to alter the outlook of his people.) But does the myth originate solely from above? Does it not also grow out of the needs of the people: partly from their pride in the struggle and partly from their feeling of insecurity and inability to guide their own destiny? In this dawn-age, myths and mythical figures are being created. Later, when the nation has won strength and independence, those national figures will no longer be needed. Then the weaving of myths will be modified to include film-actors and footballers; then a love of country will become ridiculous and Frank Sinatra will replace Charles XII.

Yugoslavia needs its myths. Let me end by saying something about the myth that gives Olga Kontić her freedom.

You might say: 'In countries where freedom is just a word, the word is used all the more often.' And, 'The repetitive method is used to create a fiction.'

But now suppose you had never seen a cat, but had learnt to call dogs cats. You would then believe that a dog was a cat, even though a cat is something quite different. In the same way you can learn to give things which are not freedom the name of freedom. What does freedom become, then, but a word without substance — a word to dazzle and mislead? In Yugoslavia the term *sloboda*, freedom, was given to so much besides the actual concept. Is it then unreasonable to carry the argument to its logical conclusion: to suppose that some of those to whom we put the question 'Is there freedom in Yugoslavia?' and who replied 'Yes, of course there's freedom' — is it unreasonable to suppose that they may have been thinking of biscuits, cinemas, tractors and candy?

Tell a man born behind bars that the people outside are dressed in the colourful clothes of prisoners because they must serve their terrible sentence, which is to struggle ceaselessly to attain perishable aims, and constantly suffer the pangs of choice and renunciation. Say to him:

'Look out at that pitiful world, where people wander in anguish trying to decide whether they dare give up A for B, or B for A, and where they're tormented by uncertainty as to whether the future will reward or punish them for their choice!'

Describe the outside world in such a way, and the man born to life-imprisonment will call our blue sky and green woods a gaol.

Tell him that he has escaped the hourly agony of decision because once in a former life he had the divine freedom to choose his present existence. He will praise the freedom that spared him the cruel blue sky and instead gave him harmonious grey walls, the glorious lack of responsibility and the safe, punctual walks between dining-hall, cell and workshop.

Freedom, whether in Sweden or Yugoslavia, is always an illusion. Perhaps we should aim at something else — something different from mere political liberty. There are after all more important things to live for.